346.73048
F923p

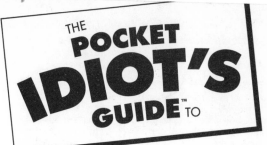
THE
POCKET
IDIOT'S
GUIDE™ TO

Trademarks

D1409655

by Robert J. Frohwein and
Gregory Scott Smith

ALPHA

A member of Penguin Group (USA) Inc.

2007

APR

*To our wives, Dana and Laura, and our children,
Michael, Lizabeth, and Scott, who put up with us as
we spent our nights and weekends writing this book.*

International Standard Book Number: 1-59257-230-8
Library of Congress Catalog Card Number: 200408620

06   05   04   8   7   6   5   4   3   2   1

Interpretation of the printing code: The rightmost number of the
first series of numbers is the year of the book's printing; the rightmost number of the second series of numbers is the number of
the book's printing. For example, a printing code of 04-1 shows
that the first printing occurred in 2004.

Printed in the United States of America

Note: This publication contains the opinions and ideas of its authors.
It is intended to provide helpful and informative material on the subject matter covered. It is sold with the understanding that the authors
and publisher are not engaged in rendering professional services
in the book. If the reader requires personal assistance or advice, a
competent professional should be consulted.

The authors and publisher specifically disclaim any responsibility for
any liability, loss, or risk, personal or otherwise, which is incurred
as a consequence, directly or indirectly, of the use and application
of any of the contents of this book.

Most Alpha books are available at special quantity discounts for
bulk purchases for sales promotions, premiums, fund-raising, or educational use. Special books, or book excerpts, can also be created to
fit specific needs.

For details, write: Special Markets, Alpha Books, 375 Hudson Street,
New York, NY 10014.

Contents

1 On Your Mark, Get Set, Go!   1
2 Making Your Mark   13
3 Rights and Wrongs with Trademarks   29
4 Locking in Your Trademark   43
5 Preparing and Filing an Application   61
6 The Examination and Registration   79
7 The Life of a Trademark   99
8 Domain Names and Trademarks   117
9 Do You Own Your Trademark?   129
10 International Trademarks   141
11 Making Money off of Trademarks   161
12 The Web and Lawyers   173

Appendixes

A Further Reading   185
B Glossary   187
  Index   195

Introduction

When you were born, your parents gave you a name. A lot went into that decision. They consulted friends and grandparents, baby naming books and even considered giving you the name of their favorite TV or movie star. But why was so much time or effort invested? Why is there not a standard name by which everyone is called?

The answer is simple—differentiation and uniqueness. You're not like everyone else. And your parents certainly couldn't have everyone come running when they called out your name. You also corrected people who said your name wrong—you were Rob, not Bob or Lizzy, not Eliza.

Congratulations. You now understand trademarks. Trademarks are simply names, designs, symbols, slogans, or other elements given to products and services for many of the same reasons that names are doled out to individuals. They're also the subjects of fierce protection by the companies who created them because many other companies would love to call their goods by similar names.

In this book, you are going to learn all that you need to know about trademarks. We'll help you understand a bit of the law around trademarks, but most important how to pick a good mark for your good or service, how to protect it, and how to stop others from stepping all over your rights.

Extras to Help You Along

This book also has useful information provided in sidebars throughout the text.

Good Counsel

This box provides simple tips to help you recognize and protect your intellectual property.

Legal-Ease

These sidebars boil down legalese into easy to understand language.

Just the Facts

This box presents fascinating stories about the trademarks.

Objections

These tips will keep you inside the boundaries of the law.

Acknowledgments

We'd like to thank Paul Dinas, Michael Koch, and Janette Lynn for their help in putting this book together.

Trademarks

On Your Mark, Get Set, Go!

In This Chapter

- Why trademarks are important
- Understanding the landscape of trademarks
- The basic rules of trademarks
- Difference from patents and copyrights

We are bombarded every day by thousands of advertisements promoting, well, just about everything. Companies are placing ads in bathrooms, on telephone poles, and even on trashcans. How are we supposed to process all of this information? The reality is that we can't. It's impossible. Companies that want to promote their goods and services are forced to convey a huge amount of information in a nanosecond. However, an extremely effective way to do this is to create and develop a name, symbol, or device to represent that good or service. Over time these companies help us to identify their goods or services through this simple, but catchy and memorable mechanism, known as a trademark. Trademarks can be legally protected so that others

can't take advantage of the investment you've made in promoting your trademark.

Trademark protection is only one form of intellectual property protection. Other types of intellectual property protection include patents and copyrights. Each of these types of protection is meant to apply to different things and provide different types of coverage. In this chapter, we're going to explain the very basics of what a trademark is. We're also going to briefly explain the differences between trademarks, patents, and copyrights.

What's in a Name?

The historical origins of the use of trademarks is, at best, quite sketchy. Some say that the early Egyptians provided the earliest confirmed use of trademarks by branding their cattle to identify ownership. Regardless as to where this concept arose, today it is obvious that we live in a world where many people understand the need for having names attributed to goods, services, and companies.

Branding

The general category of protection that trademarks fall under can be called *branding*. Companies create names and symbols to represent their goods and services so that they can build brand awareness. If branding is successful, consumers will select a company's goods or services because they recognize the name or symbol and associate positive feelings with that name or symbol.

The Different Types of Branding

Branding can be found in several forms. The most popular form is the use of a trademark or service mark. A trademark is used to identify goods (for example, tools, cars, or peanuts) and a service mark is used to identify services (for example, house-cleaning services or restaurants). The mark can be a word, a phrase, a slogan, a picture, a symbol, a shape, a logo, or a combination of any of these. In addition, other attributes, including color, font, sound, scent, and so on, can be protected by a trademark or service mark. In this book, we'll refer to all of these items generally as *marks* and some-times as *trademarks*.

Just the Facts

You might be familiar with the term **trademark** but the term **service mark** might be new to you. A reason for this might be that many people use the word trade-mark to generically refer to all forms of branding protection including trademarks, service marks, trade names, trade dress, and so on.

Trade Dress

Another form of branding is trade dress, which relates to the look and feel of a good or service. For example, the uniforms and furnishings at a Wendy's restaurant form a part of its trade dress

(that is, what you expect to see in that restaurant). In general, you can view trade dress as being broader than a trademark or service mark. For example, a company's trade dress can, and typically does, include its trademarks and service marks. While this book focuses more specifically on trademarks, you should realize that the trade dress of an organization can be protected and defended under the Lanham Act, which we describe in more detail later in this chapter.

Just the Facts

Did you know that franchises such as McDonald's and Wendy's control just about everything you encounter when you go into their restaurants? They want to convey a very specific trade dress so everything's the same from the color scheme, the uniforms, and even the straws you drink from.

Affixation and Use: Requirements for Protection

For you to gain rights to a trademark, you must affix your mark to the good you're selling or the service you're marketing. Further, you must *actually* use the mark. You can't claim a name unless you have an actual intent to use the mark in connection with the good or service.

Affixing a Mark

Trademark protection requires *affixation* of the mark. What does that mean exactly? It differs depending on whether you're offering goods or services. To gain rights in a mark, the following applies:

- **For goods.** The mark must appear on the goods, the container for the goods, or displays associated with the goods. Therefore, for example, if you're selling a toothbrush, you can have the trademark affixed to the handle.

- **For services.** The mark must be used or displayed in the sale or advertising of the services. If you're promoting your service in the newspaper, the ad should contain the trademarked name of the service (for example, Scotty's Laundromat).

Use of a Mark Is Required

Ownership of a trademark is typically based on actual use of the mark or name in commerce. That means that you cannot simply "reserve" a name because you think it sounds cool. You have to actually use or intend to use the name to identify a good or service when you're selling the goods or services. This ownership provides legal protection for the owner in the geographic area where the mark is being used and limits the protection of the mark to the category of goods or services you are offering under the mark and related categories. You can

extend this geographic territory by federally registering the mark. Also, please note though that occasionally the same name could be used for two completely different types of goods, such as Delta Airlines and Delta Faucets. We'll cover the issue of geography and to what extent related goods or services can be protected by your mark to a greater extent in Chapter 3.

Good Counsel

While you can't reserve a name because you think it's cool, you can reserve a name if you intend to actually use it in the future—this is called an intent-to-use trademark application.

Protecting Your Brand

In the United States, protection for a trademark can be found under common law (law that has developed in states through numerous court cases) or through federal law (registering with the U.S. Patent and Trademark Office and even under other federal laws like the Lanham Act). There are even some states that have a registration process. However, the common law and federal protection are the most common methods for protection of a trademark.

Just the Facts _____

> For a trademark to be federally regis-
> tered, there must be _use in commerce_,
> which means commerce between states
> or between a state and a foreign country.

State Law

Under state law, you're not required to do anything
to obtain rights to the mark you're using for your
good or service. To enjoy rights in your mark, you
must simply affix your mark to your good (like
Nike putting the swoosh symbol on its sneakers)
and then actually start selling the good. Once you
do this, you're protected under state common law
as long as nobody beat you to the punch! However,
please note that state law will only protect you in
the geographic region in which you sell your goods
or offer your services. Federal registration is necessary to gain broader national protection.

Federal Registration

In 1946, the government enacted the Lanham Act,
which, among other things, created the system necessary to allow companies to legally protect their
brands nationally and enforce their rights against
would-be infringers. The Lanham Act defined a
trademark as "any word, name, symbol, device or
any combination thereof adopted by a manufacturer

or merchant to identify his goods and distinguish them from those manufactured or sold by others."

Just the Facts

The Lanham Act was named after Fritz Garland Lanham, a congressman from Texas presiding from 1919 to 1947. Among other things, the intent of the Lanham Act is to regulate commerce by preventing deceptive and misleading use of marks in commerce and protect against unfair competition.

Registering a trademark with the U.S. Patent and Trademark Office can have the effect of expanding the geographical region of protection for that mark so that it will be protected nationwide. Geographic expansion of the protection of the mark enables brands to expand from one specific market to other markets, without the fear that another company may subsequently begin to sell a good similar to yours with a name similar to yours in that geographic region.

The U.S. Patent and Trademark Office

The U.S. Patent and Trademark Office (USPTO) is the federal agency that is responsible for reviewing applications for federal registration of a mark. The USPTO simply decides whether you meet the requirements for registration of the mark, but

this differs from whether you have the right to actually use the mark. It is quite possible that you meet the requirements to register the mark, but that another mark owner challenges your right to use that mark given their own registration. On the flip side, a valid registration permits you to stop others from using a mark that would likely confuse consumers as to the source of the origin of the goods or services.

Why Is Protection Needed?

Why is protection needed? There are really two answers to this question. On the one side is consumer protection and on the other corporate exploitation.

Consumer Protection

By providing a company with a legally protected right to a brand, the government provides a level of comfort to consumers who can identify the particular company providing goods or services by observing the brand of that particular company attached to those goods or services. Therefore, if you buy a good that carries "The Coca-Cola Company" brand, you have a certain level of comfort and knowledge about the good. You can often make a purchasing decision based simply on the fact that a company you trust produces the good. However, if any company could use that name without the permission of the Coca-Cola Company, then you might lose that level of comfort.

Corporate Exploitation

There is much more to trademarks than just permitting consumers to accurately identify the source of goods or services. Use of a world famous brand or name is a very valuable marketing tool and can create significant competitive advantages over companies with less popular brands. In addition, companies don't typically take an "order form" approach to coming up with names. They make sure the names convey an intended feeling to a consumer and they try to identify catchy names that will stick in the minds of the consumer. For example, which of the following MP3 players would you be more inclined to purchase? The RioSport or the S35S? Well, actually, they identify the same device. But although a model number (for example, S35S) may be convenient from a manufacturing and processing perspective, it just does not pique the same interest as a name like RioSport does from a marketing perspective. Some companies spend hundreds of thousands and even millions of dollars in developing, creating, and protecting their brands. Once they spend these dollars, their brands can become so valuable that consumers are willing to spend more money to buy a good marketed under a specific name.

They're Not Patents or Copyrights!

Many people lump together patents, copyrights, and trademarks. While they all have one thing in common (they're all forms of intellectual property

protection), they are not the same and should not be used interchangeably. Each is a form of legal protection covering items created by your mind.

We wanted to provide you with a quick description of what patents and copyrights are used to protect so that you can forever tell them apart from trademarks.

Copyrights

Copyrights protect the expression of an idea, and are usually referred to as *works*. These works fall into a variety of categories, including literary works (books), sound recordings (music), visuals arts (statues), performing arts (movies), and serials and periodicals (newspapers).

Copyrights provide the owner with certain exclusive rights such as the right to reproduce the work, distribute it, perform it, make a derivative work (for example, the movie version of a book), and display it.

Patents

A patent is a form of legal protection for ideas, inventions, processes, and methods. Your article about a new idea can be protected by a copyright, but the idea itself can be protected with a patent. Also, unlike a copyright, your invention is not protected the moment you conceive it and put it down on paper. Rather, you must go through the process of applying for a patent through the U.S. Patent and Trademark Office.

⚖️ **Good Counsel** _____

Your intellectual property strategy should seek to protect your company through a combination of intellectual properties—patents, trademarks, and copyrights.

Patent protection allows the owner of the patent to prevent others from doing certain things with the invention. Specifically, the patent owner can prevent others from making, using, selling, offering to sell, or importing goods or services that are covered by the patent invention. Essentially, the grant gives the inventor a monopoly in the invention for a limited period of time (while the patent is in force).

The Least You Need to Know

- Trademarks are used to identify and distinguish goods and services from competition.
- Your trademark can be protected by state or federal law, or both.
- Generally, patents protect inventions, copyrights protect expressive works, and trademarks protect names, symbols, brands, and other marks that are distinctive to your good or service.

Making Your Mark

In This Chapter

- Coming up with a great mark
- It's good to be different
- Something a bit unusual

Your name is critical. Just think of the variety of home service companies—alarm, home repair, heating and air conditioning, and other similar companies—that serve your community. Did you ever notice that most of them begin with one or more As, such as AAA Alarm Systems or AA Electricians? Of course, this is because they're listed alphabetically in the phone book and they realize that you, as the customer, start with the As and work down the list until you find someone you like.

The alphabet game is just one factor that goes into deciding what to call your company, good, or service. Other factors include what message you want to convey to customers (like quality, security, or speed) or how different you are (coming up with a

name very different from your competitors). Therefore, there's a strong marketing reason for your
name, logo, or other design that identifies your
good or service. Obviously, you need to take all
of this into consideration when you're coming up
with a mark. However, the other thing you need
to consider is whether you're going to be able to
register your mark and, possibly, stop another company from using it in the future. For this, you need
to understand what the boundaries are for registering and protecting a mark and, in this chapter, we'll
take you through those factors.

Making Your Mark Distinctive

Coming up with a good mark for your goods or
services is more of an art than a science. From a
protection standpoint, you must always remember
that a primary objective of a mark is to help consumers identify the source of the origin of goods
or services. To the extent that your mark is either
unable or incapable of doing that, then your use of
that mark will not be protected. Some marks are,
on their face, distinctive and satisfy this requirement
right from the get go. A great example is the Internet directory company Yahoo!. However, if they had
called themselves "Internet Directory Company,"
they would have had a tougher time distinguishing
themselves from every other online directory company. We're going to take you through a few types
of marks—arbitrary, fanciful, and suggestive—that
the U.S. Patent and Trademark Office (USPTO)

has decided are distinctive enough to grant registration. This means that you can register one of these types of marks as soon as you start selling the good or service in commerce (and can file an intent to use application prior to doing this as well!).

Arbitrary Marks

Yahoo! is an example of an arbitrary mark. While the founders of Yahoo! didn't dream up a new English word by which to call their company and service, they picked a word that has, frankly, nothing to do with what they do as a company. This is called an arbitrary mark. The best way to figure out whether your mark is arbitrary is to ask yourself, "could someone purchasing my good or service even get a hint of what I do from my mark?" The USPTO believes that arbitrary marks are distinctive and capable of immediate registration. The benefit is also the burden. Sometimes it seems worthwhile to convey a clearer picture to the consumer of what you're selling or doing. That's not possible if you have an arbitrary mark.

Fanciful Marks

At least with an arbitrary mark, the consumer has likely heard of the word that you've used as a mark. With "fanciful marks" you're making up a brand new word! Great examples of fanciful marks include TiVo, Xerox, and Kodak. Fanciful marks suffer from the same downside as arbitrary marks

because companies must make tremendous efforts to convey what they are selling to consumers independent of their names. On the positive side, it's very easy to identify infringers of your mark because you should be, presumably, the only one using it.

Suggestive Marks

Somewhere between Yahoo! and Internet Directory Service lies a class of marks known as *suggestive marks*. They're not completely unrelated to the good or service offered, but they're also not completely descriptive either. They merely provide the consumer with a "clue" as to what the good or service is. A great example of a suggestive mark is MasterCard. There's definitely the suggestion that you're receiving a card, but not a credit card (otherwise, it would simply be called "CreditCard").

What's the point of a suggestive mark? It's intended to convey specific meanings to the consumer. One could assume that MasterCard is intended to convey that, with this card, you'll be in control. With some strong promotion, suggestive marks can be more quickly associated by consumers with the goods or services offered by a company.

Corporate Names Versus Trademarks

As you know by now, a trademark identifies the source of the origin of goods. So can the name of your company be a trademark? Frankly, it depends on whether you utilize your company's name in

connection with selling your good or marketing your service. If your company's name is on the good, then, yes, it can also be a trademark. However, if the name of your company is just in the background and is not affixed to your good, then registration and protection is not available.

When Do I Use TM, SM, or ®?

As soon as you start using a mark in commerce—even if it's just on a local level and you never intend to register the mark, you should start affixing one of these symbols, which indicates your belief that you have rights in the mark. These symbols essentially put consumers and would-be competitors on notice. Here are the specific meanings and uses of each:

- **TM.** This indicates your belief that you possess a trademark in your mark for your goods.
- **SM.** This indicates your belief that you possess a service mark in your mark for your services.
- **®.** This indicates that you own a federal registration in your mark but it may only be used as long as the mark is affixed to goods or services that are included in the description of your registration. You should never use this symbol when an application is pending.

Where you should place them: Typically, you can position the symbol to the upper or lower right of the registered mark (for example, Google®).

What If Your Mark Is Not Inherently Distinctive?

If your mark is not arbitrary, fanciful, or suggestive, it is not considered inherently distinctive. As a result it will only be granted registration after it has achieved *secondary meaning*. The marks that would fall into this category are descriptive or misdescriptive marks, slogans, last names, and geographic terms.

What Is Secondary Meaning?

Before we get into the different categories of non-distinctive marks, it makes sense to get some understanding of the concept of secondary meaning. For a mark to have gained secondary meaning, consumers (people like us) need to recognize or mentally associate that mark with a particular source of goods or services. In our previous example, if a friend said to you, "Hey, I went online to the Internet Directory Company, and looked up the best restaurants in the city," secondary meaning would exist if you understood which internet directory service your friend referred to. Bottom line, consumers need to recognize the mark as the brand name of a *specific* company. Later, we'll describe more of the process that you need to go through to register a mark that has achieved secondary meaning.

Legal-Ease _____

The Lanham Act doesn't actually use the term **secondary meaning**. Instead, it uses the terminology that the mark "has become distinctive." However, both mean the same thing.

Descriptive Marks

Internet Directory Company is an example of a descriptive mark for a company that provides an online Internet directory. As you might expect, descriptive means that your mark actually describes the good or services. As a result, a consumer would likely have a difficult time identifying the source of the Internet service provider because most any Internet directory company would use these words to describe what they do. To gain registration of a descriptive mark, the trademark law requires that the company demonstrates that the mark has achieved secondary meaning. Therefore, when selecting a mark for your company, be careful to draw the line between a descriptive mark and a mere suggestive mark.

Is It Suggestive or Descriptive?

You might be asking yourself, "How do I figure out whether the name I have come up with is suggestive or descriptive?" You're not the only one who has asked that question! And, it's a tough one to answer.

Typically, the courts (and let's hope it doesn't come to that for you) look at a few factors to decide on which side of the fence your mark falls.

- First, how much imagination do you have to use to figure out what good or service is being offered for sale? The more imagination, the less descriptive.

- Second, would your competitors need to use the words of your mark to describe their good or service? The more the answer is yes, the more descriptive the mark is.

- Finally, have your competitors been actually using the words of your mark to describe their goods or services in the past? If this has been the case, then put another checkmark on the side of descriptiveness.

Last Names

What do Sears, Hewlett-Packard, Johnson & Johnson, and Schwab have in common? They're all the last names of the founders of these companies. Both state courts and the Lanham Act are in agreement that a mark for a company that is a last name cannot be protected or registered until it has achieved secondary meaning. Therefore, if you want to use your last name to promote your good or service, you're going to have to prove secondary meaning before you can protect or defend the mark.

So if your name is Michael Hewlett and you want to start a computer company and call it by your name, are you allowed to (given that Hewlett-Packard is a registered trademark)? This is a tough question. Generally, there's an exception in trademark law that lets you take advantage of your name in connection with a good or service you create and offer. However, courts will often make you qualify your use of your name and explicitly mention that you're not affiliated with the company that holds the other, registered mark.

Geographic Terms

What if you want to simply stick your city's name in front of a description of your services, like *Central Pennsylvania Quilts*? This gets a bit tricky, but the law says that if the geographic place is a *plausible* location for the types of goods or services being offered, then the mark is considered geographically descriptive and a demonstration of secondary meaning is required for protection and registration. Therefore, our Central Pennsylvania Quilts example would require proof of secondary meaning.

So what's tricky about that? What if the place of origin doesn't have any real connection to what is being sold? An example of this could include HAWAII for ice. If your mark falls into this category, the courts have termed your mark as "geographically deceptive misdescriptive" and, therefore, arbitrary and distinctive. Congrats— you can apply for registration.

Slogans

Here's a quick test. Name the companies that are associated with the following three slogans:

"Just do it"

"You deserve a break today"

"Don't leave home without it"

If you said Nike, McDonald's, and American Express, you're correct! Just like specific names of goods and services, companies often build sales through branding a slogan. For the same reason you were able to identify the source of the slogans, companies are able to protect a slogan—slogans can be distinctive. As you might imagine, slogans can also lean toward being descriptive. The UPS Store could not register a slogan such as "We provide mail boxes and shipping services" because it's descriptive and their competitors would need to use the same slogan to describe their businesses. Therefore, the same rules apply to this class of marks as any others— for immediate registration, an applicant needs to demonstrate that the mark is distinctive (arbitrary, fanciful or, most likely, merely suggestive).

Terms Incapable of Distinctiveness

What if you called your new bread company *Bread*? If you do, forget about seeking any protection for it. Certain terms will never be able to gain secondary meaning and, therefore, they'll never be able to be protected or registered. These terms are called

generic terms. A generic term is one that's used to describe the category of goods or services it falls into.

Change a Bad Mark Early

Love at first sound. That's the way many people think about the name they've come up with for their great new company, good, or service. The moment it rolls off their lips, they imagine the TV commercial and the introduction of their great new good with their great new name. Then, they start getting worried. What if someone else is using the name? What if someone thinks of it today and trademarks it! My business, my life will be gone.

If we've just described you, we have one word for you—*relax*! First, it is quite possible that your great name will be just fine. Second, if someone is using the name for a similar good or service as you're planning to offer, guess what? Think of a new name. The first key to successfully naming your good or service is not to get too attached to it before you make sure that you can actually use it and protect it in the way you intended.

The major lesson here: It's much easier to change a name before you've invested money into it, than after you have—no matter how much you love it.

The Forbidden Zone of Trademarks

The USPTO rejects registration of a variety of other marks on the basis that they're deceptive, scandalous, or otherwise inappropriate.

Deceptive Marks

You cannot register a mark that is considered deceptive. It's deceptive if it contains a falsity that is the reason a consumer purchases the good or service. These situations arise most often when the mark conveys some comparison to its competitors or the achievement of some status. An example of this might be *Highest Rated Beer*.

Scandalous Marks

The USPTO will not grant a registration in an immoral or scandalous mark. This rule is commonly applied when someone wants to register a sexually suggestive mark or a profanity.

Other Inappropriate Marks

You can't register a mark that …

- Incorrectly suggests an affiliation with any person (living or dead) or company (no Albert Einstein's Brain Juice).
- Directly uses someone's name, likeness, or signature without consent.
- Consists of the flag of any state, the United States, or any foreign country.

Huh? That Can Be a Trademark?

While a large percentage of marks come in the form of names or slogans, a growing number of

marks come in other forms. A good example of this
is the Artist formerly known as Prince. Why is he
called this? Because Prince changed his name to a
symbol. Once again, you need to remember that
a trademark is pretty much *anything* that helps a
consumer identify the origin of goods or services.
Therefore, as long as the mark meets the criteria of
distinctiveness, a mark can be a shape, sound, scent,
or color. A specific building can also be considered
a trademark. Let's dig a little deeper!

Stylized Marks

Many companies do not simply type in normal
text the great mark they developed. Nike. Coca-
Cola. The Home Depot. All of these companies
have developed a specific script to use when putting
their brands on their goods or services. The most
famous is the stylized script of Coca-Cola.

The style in which you present your brand can
be subject to trademark protection. As a result,
another company can be prevented from using
the same stylized method if it would confuse a
customer as to the source of the origin of the
goods or services. You can imagine the confusion
if Dana Cola was scripted in the same way that
Coca-Cola is.

Designs

The most common form of mark after a simple
name (and the stylized form of that name) is a
design or logo. A logo is a symbol that's used in

connection with a good or service and they require the same element of distinctiveness to be registered.

Shapes

Shapes of a good can serve as a trademark. The classic example of this is the shape of the old Coca-Cola bottles that were recently reintroduced by the Coca-Cola Company. Like any mark, the shape has to be inherently distinctive or it must gain secondary meaning over time. However, there's a hitch. To receive protection, the shape also has to be *nonfunctional*. If the shape of the good improves the performance of the good, then the shape cannot be subject to trademark protection.

An example of this might be a redesigned barrel of a gun that enables better aim at a target. The gun company that created the improved barrel shape could not receive a trademark in the shape of the barrel because it serves a functional purpose—better accuracy. However, the company could benefit from their invention by applying for a patent.

Sounds

A specific sound can be associated with a particular good or services. One of the most well-known examples of this type of trademark is the three chime sound for the TV network, NBC.

Scents

Scents can be registered. The nonfunctionality requirement exists with respect to scents as well, so scents of perfumes cannot be registered as trademarks (because they serve the purpose of improving the smell of the person wearing the perfume). Therefore, a scent associated with some other good (like scented sewing thread) could be registered.

Colors

An increasing number of companies are associating specific colors with their good or service. The United Parcel Service (UPS) has received a registered trademark in the color brown in connection with shipping services. Once again, it's critical that the color not serve a particular function.

How can a color be functional? It can serve psychological purposes, like getting you to eat a meal more quickly in a restaurant and, thus, get the tables "turned over" more quickly. In the event it does serve a functional purpose, then registration and protection is not available. The other thing that the USPTO has decided is that color marks are never inherently distinctive, so secondary meaning must be proven.

Buildings

The shape of a building can be registered as a trademark. Once again, it needs to meet the tests for nonfunctionality and distinctiveness. As a result,

owners of a mark in a building can prohibit others from using the design to promote some other good or service. A good example might be a company that leverages the design of the Empire State Building to promote their company Empire Cleaners.

The Least You Need to Know

- A mark needs to be distinctive or gain secondary meaning to be registered and protected.
- A mark can come in the form of a name, slogan, or a variety of other forms such as colors, shapes, sounds, and scents.
- Marks that are generic, deceptive, or scandalous cannot be registered.

Chapter **3**

Rights and Wrongs with Trademarks

In This Chapter

- Your rights as a mark owner
- The ins and outs of infringement
- Safe use of another's mark

Have you ever been in a restaurant and asked for a Coke and had the server say, "Is Pepsi ok?" If so, you've had a trademark protection experience. The server is not asking you because he's afraid you don't like Pepsi. The server is asking you because he's afraid he'll get in trouble if he doesn't. Pepsi doesn't want its good passed off as a Coke in restaurants. So what's the big deal? Companies spend millions every year to ensure that their brands portray exactly what they want them to portray. If they don't, then these companies are wasting their money and potentially letting others generate sales thanks to their hard work.

Trademarks can be extremely valuable. In many instances, the name of your good can be the sole reason that someone is purchasing it and, perhaps, willing to pay a premium for it. In this chapter, we help you understand exactly why obtaining and maintaining trademarks is so valuable. We'll also outline when you can and when you cannot use someone else's trademark.

Why You Should Bother with Trademarks

So what's all the fuss? Why should you make such an effort to ensure that you have a registerable, protectable trademark?

Just the Facts

In 2003, *Business Week* considered Coca-Cola the most valuable brand in the world with a value of $70.45 billion, with Microsoft as the second highest at $65.17 billion.

Trademarks can be worth a tremendous amount of money. For some companies, the brand is the most valuable asset of the entire company. This especially happens in industries in which the good that the company is selling is not that differentiable from the goods of its competitors. While some might argue that Coke is the best cola in the world,

the reality is that someone could invent or produce a cola that tastes better. Some would argue that better goods are already on the market. However, Coke has invested countless dollars into supporting its brand and making sure that everyone is aware of its existence.

So What Are Your Rights as a Mark Owner?

They say imitation is the finest form of flattery. That might be true, but imitation is a surefire way to get you sued when it comes to trademark law. Once a trademark owner has taken the steps necessary to protect a mark, the user of a mark that creates a *likelihood of confusion* is considered to be committing trademark infringement. A likelihood of confusion exists when consumers think that the offending goods or services are sourced from or associated with the valid trademark owner. Therefore, if someone other than Nike, Inc. puts the Nike swoosh on a pair of sweat pants, would consumers think that either Nike produces the good or someone affiliated with Nike does? You better believe it.

Trademark infringement comes in many different varieties. Some infringement is absolutely clear— the identical mark is being affixed to the identical goods or services. In these instances, it's much easier to prove a likelihood of confusion. However, some infringement is less obvious. Someone might

be using a similar type of mark on a related type of goods and services.

Figuring Out the Likelihood of Confusion

When questionable situations arise, a variety of factors must be considered to figure out whether there is a likelihood of confusion and, as a result, infringement! These factors can relate to the similarity between the actual marks, the makeup of the market to whom you're selling, the geographic region you're selling in, and what goods and services your company and the offending company offer. Let's take you through some of them.

How Similar Are the Marks?

As you might imagine, the first test is to actually compare the two marks from a variety of perspectives including how they look, sound, and what they actually mean.

- **Sight.** Do the marks from an overall perspective look similar? If so, the allegedly infringing mark may confuse consumers. Therefore, things such as a similar style in which they're written and an identical number of letters in the names might be enough to demonstrate infringement.

- **Sound.** Say the two marks out loud. Do they sound the same? What if one educational software company called themselves

LMN and you wanted to call your educational software company ElleEmmEnn? There would be a likelihood of confusion because they sound identical.

- **Meaning.** Say what you mean and mean what you say. The meaning behind marks might lead to a likelihood of confusion. A good example of this might be a new roofing company called Thunder entering the territory that Lightning Roofing has called home for many years.

Go to the Streets!

Evidence of actual confusion by regular folks can be a powerful tool in proving that there's confusion (or that there's not!). One way to accomplish this is through a survey. The results of that survey (and, obviously not just asking your mother) can be introduced in your effort to prove or disprove confusion.

Did You Spend a Million?

Courts generally believe the more consumers spend on a good or service, the less likely they're going to be confused between two, otherwise similar, marks. It's hard to imagine that you would spend a significant amount of money without doing your homework and learning from whom you're buying the goods.

How Unsophisticated Are the Consumers?

Some goods draw more sophisticated customers (high tech gadgets) and others draw a less sophisticated crowd (potato chips). Courts figure that less sophisticated consumers are more likely to be confused by similar marks.

Are Similar Goods or Services Being Offered?

Can you start an ice cream shop called Nike Ice Cream? We wish there was a clear-cut answer to this question. The reality is that your purchase of Nike Ice Cream will not decrease Nike's sales of running shoes (in fact, it might increase it as everyone needs to work off those extra calories!). It used to be that the courts wouldn't support a case of infringement if the goods or services were completely unrelated. However, that has changed.

Famous Marks

Basically, there are those marks that are considered famous throughout the country. Many of them have popped up in this book, such as Microsoft, Coke, McDonald's, and Nike. If you own a famous mark (and if you do, you must be a very rich person), then use of that mark in connection with any good or service, might be dilutive to your brand. Therefore, another's use of that mark could decrease the value that you have worked so hard to create. A great example is the Nike Ice Cream Shop. If Nike has spent 30 plus years building a brand focused on athletics and exercise, your use of

it in connection with an ice cream shop might counter everything they've tried to create.

Nonfamous Marks

If your mark falls into this category, don't feel bad! Almost all marks do. Obviously, it wouldn't make sense if the protection you received for your mark only related to the specific goods or services that you offer. In other words, if you sell shaving cream under a specific mark, it wouldn't be appropriate for someone to start selling razors under the same mark as you—clearly they would be attempting to confuse customers and take advantage of the value you've created in your brand. The test is simple— would the public reasonably think that the goods are being offered by the same company or that there's some relationship between the two companies? If so, the company that took your mark has created a likelihood of confusion and is infringing. There are a variety of ways to show a relationship between two sets of goods—not only that the goods relate directly to each other (the shaving example), but the relationship could be established because they serve the same market (the elderly) or are sold in the same store (nutritional store).

The Crime Scene–Geographic Issues

One of the most critical factors in deciding whether there's been infringement is geography. As we've mentioned, federal registration protects you everywhere in the United States. What that means

is that you can stop someone from using a mark that will create a likelihood of confusion anywhere in the United States. When state rights get mixed in, however, things get more complicated.

> **Good Counsel** _____
>
> Federal registration has the effect of putting everyone on notice about your mark. Therefore, someone can't claim that they innocently infringed your rights!

What If Someone Has State Rights to the Mark First?

If Ed had used a mark in a particular part of a state and then Dave came along and federally registered the same mark, what would happen? Ed could continue to use the mark in the geographic area where he had been actually using the mark and Dave would be able to enjoy use of the mark everywhere other than that geographic area. However, if Ed started using the mark in the geographic area after Dave filed his application with the U.S. Patent and Trademark Office (USPTO), Ed could be stopped from using it entirely.

Battling for Territorial Rights

What if both Ed and Dave were using the same mark in two different areas and neither federally registers? No harm, no foul. Basically, the two can

easily co-exist with one another. Now, what if Dave and Ed want to start expanding their empires and they both want to expand into the same area? Essentially, it's a race. Whoever gets there first and starts to actually use the mark in connection with the sale of their goods or services first gets dibs on protection for the mark.

Objections

The previous examples assumed that the parties are acting in good faith and didn't have knowledge of the other person's mark before they started using it. Therefore, if you hear about a hot new company, don't start using their mark in your territory for hopes of a big payout one day when they come to town!

What Has the Internet Done to Us?!

Is there any such thing as offering a good only in one geographic territory anymore? After all, with the Internet, someone in Vineland, New Jersey can sell goods in Palm Beach Gardens, Florida with the click of a button. Of course, there are still many local businesses with legitimate rights focused only in one area. However, to the extent that a mark has become known nationally through advertising, press, and other means, it is a hard argument to say that there's any geographic limitation.

The Cease and Desist Letter

If after reading this chapter, you're ready to go out and fight because you think someone is infringing your mark, you should take a few immediate steps before you start walking down to the courthouse and filing your suit. First, it is quite possible that the person who is infringing your mark is doing so innocently. As a result, you should send the person a letter that indicates that you own the mark, that you noticed their use of the mark, and that you are requesting that they cease and desist from further use of the mark. Many times this will solve the problem without expending a tremendous amount of money on an attorney. We have included a sample cease and desist letter here for your reference.

> Dear Mr.:
>
> Remodel Clothing, Inc. manufactures and distributes clothing products throughout the United States and other countries under the registered trademark JACKHAMMER. Remodel Clothing owns a United States of America Certificate of Trademark Registration No. 100000 for the trademark JACKHAMMER for this mark as used in connection with its goods.
>
> Recently, in a search of the U.S. Patent and Trademark Office (USPTO) records, we noticed your pending Trademark Application Serial No. 76/ for HACKHAMMER, filed on March 31, 2004 for clothing. A copy of the application details is enclosed for your reference. Your use of the "HACKHAMMER" mark in connection with

goods is confusingly similar to Remodel Clothing's JACKHAMMER trademarks.

Remodel Clothing is assuming that your use of the "HACKHAMMER" mark is not an intentional effort to confuse your products with ours. However, we must point out that Remodel Clothing has been using the JACKHAMMER trademark on clothing for more than ten (10) years and has established valuable goodwill in its trademark, including these many years of quality production and extensive advertising and distribution of goods under the trademark. This has resulted in the JACKHAMMER brand of clothing becoming well-known and famous.

We must insist that you immediately agree to refrain from future use of the HACKHAMMER trademark, generally and in connection with your clothing products. While Remodel Clothing prefers to handle all disputes in a friendly manner, Remodel Clothing does take all unauthorized uses of its trademark seriously and is ready to enforce its rights in every lawful manner.

If you have any questions, please contact us to discuss this matter. Otherwise, we look forward to receiving your written assurance in the next two (2) weeks that you will refrain from future use of the mark HACKHAMMER in the manner that is confusingly similar to Remodel Clothing's trademark JACKHAMMER, and that you will change your packaging, labeling, and advertising materials so that they do not include the confusingly similar mark.

Respectfully,

You should provide the offending party some time
period—perhaps 15 or 30 days to respond to your
requests. If you do not receive a response to your
letter, then consult a trademark attorney about tak-
ing further action to protect your rights.

When Can You Use Someone Else's Mark?

Throughout this book, we've been referring to the
federally registered trademarks of a number of
companies—Microsoft, Coke, Nike, McDonald's,
and American Express, just to name a few. Should
our publisher be worried? Absolutely! (Just kid-
ding.) There are certain times when use of
another's trademark is fine:

- **Good comparisons.** You're permitted
  to use another company's trademark in connection with comparing your good against
  a competitor's. Of course, you need to be
  truthful in your comparison. Also, it is
  important to explicitly state that you're
  not the owner of the mark and who is (for
  example, "Nike is a registered trademark
  of Nike, Inc.").

- **Repairing damaged goods.** There's a huge
  second market in many goods, such as electronics, automobiles, and lots of mechanical
  products (like bikes). You're permitted to
  fix up these goods and then market them
  under the original trademark provided that
  you indicate who you are, that you're not
  affiliated with the company that owns the

trademark, and that the goods are reconditioned. For example, you could buy an old Panasonic stereo, fix it up, and offer it for sale.

- **Resale of trademarked goods.** If you're a reseller of a trademarked good, it's presumed that you're able to use the trademark to promote the fact that you sell the good. This rule also applies to companies that repair or make replacement parts for trademarked goods.

Hey, Are You Making Fun of *Me*?

Companies that own famous marks are always the subjects of ridicule. Sometimes, people use a company's mark to come out with goods that parody the company. A good example was Garbage Pail Kids, a take-off on Cabbage Patch Kids. So does a parody constitute trademark infringement? If you think about it, why would a company make fun of their own goods? The answer is they wouldn't. And if they wouldn't make fun of themselves, then a consumer wouldn't be likely to believe that the mark owner was the source of the parody. Therefore, many forms of parody have been allowed by the courts. However, the key to a successful, non-infringing parody is that the parody is supposed to create a distinction in a consumer's mind between the actual good and the joke. Therefore, tread carefully and make sure you discuss your parody

concept carefully with a trademark attorney before you use another company's protected mark.

Just the Facts

Inspired by a company that parodied them (NFFL Fro-Set), NFL football card maker Pro-Set (maker of NFL Pro-Set) decided to enter into the baseball card market in 1992 with *Flopps*, a parody on Topps and Major League Baseball. Pro-Set found Major League Baseball unhappy with the effort and Pro-Set quickly ceased production to quell potential litigation.

The Least You Need to Know

- As a trademark owner, you're protected from companies that seek to use your trademark in a way that creates a likelihood of confusion.

- Other than for famous marks, trademark owners are generally protected from similar trademarks affixed to goods or services that are reasonably related to their goods or services.

- There are a variety of instances when it is permissible to use another company's trademark.

Locking in Your Trademark

In This Chapter

- Trademark ownership versus registration
- How to register a trademark
- The rights of an owner of a registered trademark
- Classification of trademarks
- Ownership in a mark you have not used yet

The registration of a trademark is not the same as owning rights in a trademark. Owning rights in a trademark occurs when you use the trademark in commerce prior to anyone else. Such ownership is typically limited on a geographic basis. For example, if you use a trademark for a sanitation business in Paducah, Kentucky, your ownership rights are limited to that geographic area. Registering a trademark is a process whereby the U.S. government grants to you the right to prevent others from using your mark or similar and confusing marks anywhere in the nation.

Can a trademark be registered just by asking? No. You will learn that the process of registering a trademark also includes an examination as to whether you actually have rights in the trademark. In addition, the registration process allows the rest of the world to express their opinion regarding your rights in and to the trademark. Wow, I bet you did not realize how much of an effect registering a trademark would have.

There are different kinds of trademark applications and registrations. The type of application you file will depend on what you have done with the trademark in the past (for example, whether you have used the trademark or do you just intend to use the trademark). The type of registration for the trademark will depend on how unique the trademark is, how closely the trademark resembles or describes the goods or services with which it will be used, and how closely the trademark resembles other trademarks that are in use.

Legal-Ease

The principle register and the supplemental register are two different types of trademark registrations and have different rights associated with them.

In this chapter, we describe the overall process of registering a trademark, what the requirements are for obtaining a registration, and how you can apply for registration of a trademark. In addition, you

will learn a few trademark guru terms such as *principle register*, *supplemental register*, and *trademark classification*.

Trademark Rights Versus Registration

As we have already mentioned, within the United States, trademark rights begin when you actually start using a trademark. Thus, once you sell a product or offer a service under a trademark name, you instantly create trademark rights. These rights are referred to as common law rights.

The rights that you have in a trademark under common law are limited to the geographic area in which you use the trademark. For example, if you begin selling grills or cookers in the state of Georgia under the name of Sike's Cookers, you immediately have trademark rights for that trademark in Georgia. If another person begins to market a different grill in the state of Texas without any knowledge of the activity in Georgia, they would not be infringing your trademark rights. If the person in Texas tried to sell the grills in Georgia, that person would then be violating your trademark rights.

The common law rights in trademarks can be a bit frustrating when you want to pick a trademark for your company. For example, if you want to start using a trademark, it makes good sense to conduct a search to determine if anyone else is using the

mark. However, because trademark rights begin upon use of the mark, it can be quite a task to determine if anyone in the entire country has already used the mark. After all, this is a big country.

U.S. law allows you to federally register your trademarks. The advantage of a federal registration is that it provides nationwide use of the trademark. Thus, once your trademark is federally registered, anyone who uses the mark anywhere in the United States will be infringing your trademark—that is assuming that they did not use the trademark before you. Therefore, even though you have rights in a trademark in one area, you do not have rights to that mark nationwide unless you first register the mark federally. If someone else used the mark prior to you and did not register the mark federally, their rights will be limited to the geographic region in which they used the mark.

The Registration Process

So you have decided that you have a trademark that you want to register. Where do you begin? Well, the process of registering a trademark begins upon filing an application for registration. The registration process can be viewed as including four stages:

- Preparing and filing the application
- Examination of the application
- Publication of the trademark for opposition
- Issuance of a registration certificate

The Preparation and Filing Stage

In Chapter 5 we will describe the details of a trademark application and how you can file an application with the U.S. Patent and Trademark Office (USPTO). In general, an application for a trademark includes the following items:

- The identity of the person or entity applying for registration
- A description of the trademark
- A statement regarding how the trademark is being or will be used
- A correspondence address
- A filing fee
- A specimen
- An authorized signature

The Examination Stage

The examination stage involves a review of the application for correctness and determining whether the trademark is suitable for registration. We describe this stage in more detail in Chapter 6. But for now, you should know that the examination is carried out by an examining attorney who works for the USPTO. The examination process includes the following steps:

- Reviewing the application for errors
- Determining whether the description of the goods or services to be associated with the trademark is acceptable

- Conducting a search for similar trademarks for use with similar goods or services
- Determining whether the trademark should be registered in view of the search results

The Publication Stage

Once examination is completed and the USPTO determines that the trademark is suitable for registration, the trademark and the description of the trademark is published in the *Official Gazette*. This publication allows others to review the trademark and determine whether the registration of the trademark would have a negative impact on their business. If so, a party can oppose the registration. The activities that occur during the publication stage can range from simply waiting for the publication time period to expire to a long drawn-out battle with another party. This process is described in more detail Chapter 5.

 Legal-Ease

The *Official Gazette,* or the *Trademark Official Gazette* is a publication by the U.S. government that lists, among other things, the trademarks and service marks, as well as their description of uses. The last five issues of the *Trademark Official Gazette* can be viewed online at www.uspto.gov/web/trademarks/tmog.

The Issuance Stage

Ah, you have made it through the first three stages, now what? Well, for all your hard work and dedication, the USPTO issues you a nicely bound trademark registration certificate that you can hang on your wall. But are you done? Not quite. There continue to be ongoing obligations for a person with a registered trademark. The details of these obligations are described in Chapter 7; in general, these requirements include:

- Continuing to use the trademark
- Renewing the trademark periodically
- Policing the use of the trademark by people that you allow to use the trademark
- Making sure that others are not infringing upon your trademark by using similar or identical marks

Is It a Good or Is It a Service?

There are two broad categories of trademarks—goods or services. And although we use the term trademark throughout this book to describe marks that fall into either category, in actuality, two different terms are used to describe these trademarks. The term *trademark* is generally used to describe a mark that is associated with goods. The term *service mark* is used to describe a mark that is associated with services.

Is your specific mark a trademark or a service mark? The answer to this question depends on how you are using the mark. Answering the following questions will help you determine whether your mark should be a trademark or a service mark.

- Is your mark being used to identify a product? For instance, are you putting the mark on a product, packaging for a product, advertisements for the product, manuals or literature to be included with the product, or tags or stickers to be placed on the product or packaging for the product? If the answer to these questions is yes, then your mark is being used as a trademark.

- Is your mark being used to identify a service that is provided to others? If the answer to this question is yes, then your mark is being used as a service mark.

- Is your mark being used to identify a particular product, such as a computer or a home appliance for which you also provide installation services? If the primary purpose of the mark is to identify the goods, and the service being provided is just an expected part of the sale of the goods, then the mark is a trademark.

- What happens if your mark is being used to identify a service, but along with that service you provide products? For example, suppose you use the mark Top Hat Entertainment as a mark indicating the service of promoting

young musicians and assisting them in obtaining gigs. In conjunction with this service, suppose you also sell Top Hat Entertainment clothing. Is your mark a service mark or a trademark? Basically, if the service is a bona fide service, and the sale of the clothing is only incidental to the service, then the mark is still a service mark.

Examples of trademarks that are used for goods include the following:

- PING I3 for golf clubs and golf bags
- BIC for lead pencils and marking pens
- BIG MAC for two all beef patties, special sauce, lettuce, cheese, pickles, onions on a sesame seed bun

Examples of service marks include the following:

- MERRY MAIDS for commercial and residential cleaning services
- AOL.COM for providing users access to networks

A single mark can be registered as a trademark and as a service mark. Examples of such trademarks include the following:

- Coca-Cola for a carbonated drink and for retail stores
- Panasonic for consumer electronics and for servicing or repair of consumer electronics

- Glenayre for paging equipment and servicing or installation of voice and data communication equipment

Every Trademark Needs Class

Every registered trademark is placed into at least one classification. As we have already discussed, a trademark can be used as a trademark for goods, or a service mark for services. However, there are many classifications within these two uses in which a mark can be registered.

Classifications are used to group marks for like goods and services into a single class. The purpose for classifying trademarks is not to limit or extend your rights in using the mark. Instead, the classification system is simply a convenience for the USPTO. One thing for sure, the classification system is not a convenience for the person filing an application for registration. In fact, if your trademark falls into more than one classification, you actually have to pay additional money to register the trademark. The application fee for registration is based on the number of classes to which your trademark applies. Thus, for each class of goods or services, you will have to pay a separate registration fee.

Determining which classification your trademark should be registered in can be a daunting task. The USPTO publishes a manual called *Acceptable*

Identification for Goods and Services Manual. In this manual there are more than 10,000 different classification entries for goods and more than 2,500 classification entries for services. On top of this, from time to time they add new classifications and delete some of the existing classifications.

However, do not fret because we have good news for you about trademark classifications. The classification system is primarily a convenience for the USPTO, so they make classification of the trademark convenient for you. If you don't identify the correct classification for your particular trademark, they will assign it to the appropriate classification or identify additional classifications in which your trademark should be registered, or both.

The following list provides examples of trademark classifications. These examples are taken directly out of the *Acceptable Identification of Goods and Services Manual.*

- International Class Number 031 is used for trademarks associated with dog food.
- International Class Number 028 is used for trademarks associated with golf clubs, as well as golf club head covers. So if a trademark TIGER PROTECTOR was filed for the golf club head that follows Tiger Woods around, it would be registered in this class.
- International Class Number 015 is used for trademarks associated with guitar strings.
- International Class Number 021 is used for trademarks associated with saltshakers.

> **Just the Facts** _____
>
> You can access the *Acceptable Identi-fication of Goods and Services Manual* at www.uspto.gov/web/offices/tac/doc/gsmanual/. This Internet address also includes a search engine to help you iden-tify a classification for your trademark based on keywords that describe your product.

Registering a Mark Before You Use It

You might file three different types of applications for registration. The first type of application is used when you have already begun use of the mark. This is referred to as a use-based application. The second type of application is an intent-to-use trade-mark application. The third type of application is one that is based on a trademark registration from another country. In this section we are going to focus on the intent-to-use trademark application.

Suppose you have come up with a new product idea that you are certain is going to be a smash hit, even more so than the Pet Rock or the Chia Pet. In addition, suppose you have identified a perfect name for the product. As you have learned, rights in a trademark vest upon use of the trademark. However, in this situation you realize that it might be quite a while before you are actually going to have products to deliver to customers. This puts

you in quite a dilemma. For example, you don't want to spend hundreds or thousands of dollars on packaging for the product just to find out the day before your first big shipment that someone else is using the mark. What do you do?

The USPTO allows you to file an application for the registration of a trademark that you intend to use. The requirements for filing an intent-to-use application are similar to those for filing a use-based application with the following differences. When filing the intent-to-use application, you must provide a statement in the application indicating that you have a bona fide intent to use the trademark. The intent-to-use trademark application will go through the same examination and publication processes as the use-based application. Upon completion of the examination, the USPTO will provide a notice of allowance. However, prior to issuing a certificate of registration, you must submit a specimen indicating how the trademark is being used and file a Statement of Use. The Statement of Use is a written and signed statement indicating that you have now begun use of the trademark.

The Statement of Use can only be filed after the USPTO has provided you with a notice of allowance. After a notice of allowance has been provided, you have six months to file a Statement of Use. If you have not used the trademark during this period of time, you can file for a six-month extension. In fact, you can file for up to five six-month extensions of time for a total of three years

from the date that the notice of allowance was provided. Of course every extension of time, as well as filing a Statement of Use, requires the payment of a fee. If you have not used the trademark for three years after the notice of allowance, the application becomes abandoned.

The Principal Versus Supplemental Register

In general, an application for registration of a trademark is for registration on the principle register. If it is determined that your trademark is distinctive, then you may register your trademark on the principle register. However, if the USPTO refuses to register a mark on the principle register, you might be able to register your mark on the supplemental register. The rights available to you regarding your trademark registration are different depending on whether your trademark is on the principle or the supplemental register.

Your Rights on the Principle Register

When your trademark is registered on the principle register, you have the following rights:

- Your registration serves as notice throughout the United States that you are the owner of the trademark.

- You can use the ® symbol with your trademark.

- You can prevent others from using your trademark or a confusingly similar trademark anywhere in the United States unless they used the trademark prior to your first use.

- After five years of continuous use of the trademark, your trademark becomes incontestable which means that the registration can no longer be challenged based on someone else's prior use of the trademark or descriptiveness.

- You have the right to file a lawsuit for trademark infringement in a federal court.

- If you are successful in a lawsuit against an infringer, you can obtain increased statutory damages.

- You can use the power of the federal government to prevent goods that contain infringing marks from being imported into the United States.

Your Rights on the Supplemental Register

If registration of your trademark on the principle register is not allowed, you still have the opportunity to register your mark on the supplemental register. To be registered on the supplemental register, your trademark must be "capable" of distinguishing your goods or services, even though the mark might not currently do so.

If your trademark is registered on the supplemental register, you are still able to file a lawsuit for trademark infringement in a federal court. In addition, you can still use the ® symbol along with your trademark. However, the other rights provided through registration on the principle register are not available to you.

The supplemental register generally includes two categories of trademarks:

- Trademarks that have been registered in foreign countries but that have not yet been used in the United States.
- Trademarks that are not distinctive.

Changing from the Supplemental to the Principle Register

After a trademark has been registered on the supplemental register, you can file a request to have the registration moved to the principle register once the trademark becomes distinctive through extensive use, or after the trademark has been on the supplemental register for five years.

Foreign Trademarks

As we mentioned previously, there are three types of registrations: use based, intent to use, and registration based on a registration or application in another country. So let's briefly examine the topic of foreign trademarks.

Trademarks can be registered in virtually any country in the world. Generally, registration of a trademark in a particular country only provides protection for that mark in that country. This is certainly true in the United States. Thus, to obtain protection for your trademark in other countries, you must file for registration in each country. The details of registering a trademark in a foreign country, as well as typical concerns for foreign registrations, are provided in Chapter 10. However, for purposes of registering a trademark in the United States, you need to be aware of certain rights that you have with regard to foreign registrations.

Good Counsel

If you are going to pick a trademark, you should conduct a search to determine if the trademark is being used by others. You should also consider searching to determine if the trademark is being used in other countries and whether or not the trademark can still be registered in the United States based on the use of the trademark in foreign countries.

In general, a person that has registered a trademark in another country can file an application for registration of that mark in the United States. If the foreign trademark is not currently being used in the United States, registration of the trademark will be limited to the supplemental register.

However, if the trademark is being used in the United States, the trademark can be registered on the principle register. In addition, if the application for registration in the United States was filed within certain time limits, or through filing under certain treaties, the priority date of use within the foreign countries can be used to establish priority of use within the United States.

The Least You Need to Know

- The registration of a trademark can establish ownership in the trademark; however, you can still own a trademark that is not registered.

- To register a mark, it must be classified as a trademark or service mark, and must be further classified within these categories.

- A single mark can be registered as both a trademark and a service mark, as well as in several classifications.

- Even if you can't register your mark on the principle register because your mark is not distinctive, the mark can become distinctive over a period of time by using the mark.

- You can register a trademark that you are currently using, or one that you intend to use.

Preparing and Filing an Application

In This Chapter

- The preparation of the trademark application
- The information you must have to file a trademark application
- The requirements for the various types of trademark applications
- Filing a trademark application electronically

The first stage in the process of registering a trademark is preparing and filing an application for registration. This process is where you identify what your trademark is and define what products or services will be associated with the trademark. This task is not an overly complex one; however, as you read on you will learn that it is very important to get it right the first time.

In this chapter, we walk you through the process of preparing a trademark application and then filing the application with the U.S. Patent and Trademark Office (USPTO). The USPTO is doing a pretty good job at keeping up with technology trends without shutting the door in the face of those who are not comfortable working with computers and technology. Thus, today a trademark application can be filed either electronically, or the good old-fashioned way, by using the U.S. Post Office. We describe each of these filing techniques, as well as the specific application requirements for each filing technique.

So get your pencil and trademark in hand and let's get going on the preparation of your trademark application!

The Trademark Application

The trademark application is not complex. However, you certainly need to know what you are doing when preparing the application. But before we get into the filing process, let's first go through the preparation requirements for a trademark application.

The Must-Haves

As we have mentioned already, there are three different types of trademark applications: the use-based application, the intent-to-use application, and the

foreign registration-based application. The good news is that for the most part, these applications are very similar.

Regardless of the type of trademark application that you are preparing, your application will at least require the following information:

- The applicant information or the identity of the person or entity applying for registration
- The mark information including a description of the trademark
- A statement regarding how the trademark is being or will be used
- A correspondence address
- A filing fee
- A specimen
- An authorized signature

Let's go through these items in more detail.

The applicant information. The applicant is not necessarily the person who is preparing the trademark application. The applicant is the person who is the owner of the trademark. Of course the applicant does not have to be a person, the applicant can be an individual, a corporation, a partnership, or any of a variety of different legal entities. Depending on the type of applicant, the applicant

information can vary. For an individual, the applicant information includes:

- The full name of the applicant (last name, first name, and middle initial if any)
- The applicant's entity type, which is "individual"
- The applicant's country of citizenship
- Address or PO Box, including street, city, state, country, and zip code
- Phone number, fax number, and e-mail address if available.

If more than one individual owns the trademark, this information should be provided for both of the individuals. This information varies slightly for other entity types. For example, if the applicant is a corporation, the entity type changes to "corporation" and the country of citizenship is replaced by the state or country of incorporation. If the applicant is a partnership, the entity type is "partnership" and the country of citizenship is replaced by the state or country under whose laws the partnership is organized. In addition, for a partnership applicant, the name and citizenship of one of the individual general partners or the name and state or country of incorporation of any general partner that is a corporation is required.

Mark information. A trademark can take on many different forms. The broadest form is simple block lettering. The block lettering form seeks to protect the words themselves. However, the trademark might

include stylized formats, colors, logos, sounds, pictures, or any combination of any of these elements. The application includes a description of the trademark. If the trademark includes color, you should list the portions of the mark that are in color and the corresponding color for each portion. For stylized marks, the best method to describe the mark is through a drawing. The drawing can identify the particular shapes of the trademark and different shading techniques can be used to indicate various colors.

The mark information might include a disclaimer for certain portions of the mark. For example, if your trademark includes common words, you might want to disclaim those words. For instance, suppose your trademark is Kellogg's Frosted Flakes, it might prove difficult to obtain protection of the "Frosted Flakes" portion because it is descriptive. Thus, you can state that "no claim is made to the exclusive right to use Frosted Flakes apart from the mark as shown." The disclaimer has the effect of narrow-ing your rights, but can also help to speed up the process of getting your mark registered. If Kellogg's did not include such a disclaimer, the examining attorney might have rejected the mark based on similar marks using the words "Frosted Flakes" or Kellogg's might have been faced with opposition from other cereal manufactures.

If your trademark includes foreign words, you need to provide the English translation for those words. For example, the description for the registered trademark "La Casa Blanca" includes the following statement: The foreign wording in the mark translates into English as "The White House."

Each variation of the trademark requires a separate trademark application. For example, if you want to obtain a registration for your company name and logo, you can include both the name and logo in one application, the name alone in another application, and the logo alone in a third application.

It is important to accurately describe your trademark in the application. If you make an error in the description you might be required to file a new application with the corrected description.

Good Counsel

The filing date of a trademark application is very important because it establishes conclusive evidence of your first use of the mark. This is especially important in intent-to-use trademark applications. If your application is rejected and you must file another application, someone may use your trademark in the interim period and obtain rights in your trademark.

Use of the trademark. The application should describe how the trademark is, or will be, used. You should enter the common commercial name for the specific goods and/or services associated with the trademark. This is a tricky part of the application process. You need to describe the use with enough detail to satisfy the examining attorney but, if you use too much detail, you could end up limiting the strength of your mark. For example, the following

descriptions would be sufficient: "computer software for accounting purposes" or "shirts, pants, and shoes." However, a description such as "internet services" would be considered too broad and not only would the examining attorney reject the description, such a broad description may also have the result of you not obtaining a filing date.

In identifying the goods or services (or both), you should also include the international classification number in which you want the trademark to be registered. This is not mandatory because if you omit the international classification number, or use an incorrect number, the examining attorney will amend the application to include the correct number.

Just the Facts

Although the classification for a U.S. trademark registration is called an "international classification," your trademark application is only for protection in the United States. The term "international" is used because the United States uses the worldwide classification system.

Correspondence address. As the applicant, you can list yourself as the person to receive correspondence regarding your application. If you use an attorney to file your trademark application, you should list the name of the attorney. When listed, all communication from the USPTO regarding

your trademark application will only be directed to the listed attorney, not the applicant. You may list more than one attorney on your application. However, correspondence will only be sent to the attorney listed as the *correspondent attorney*. You can change this information after the initial filing.

The correspondence address should include the mailing address, telephone number, facsimile number if available, and e-mail address if available. The USPTO prefers to send correspondence to the applicant's attorney via e-mail.

If you are residing outside of the United States, you can appoint a domestic representative, although this is not required. If you provide the name and address of a domestic representative rather than an attorney, all correspondence from the USPTO will be delivered to the domestic representative. You can identify both an attorney and a domestic representative. In this situation, correspondence will still be sent to your attorney.

The filing fee. The filing fee is based on the number of classes in which the trademark will be registered. You can identify multiple classes for a single mark in a single application. It is important to understand that the filing fee is a nonrefundable processing fee for the application—the fee is not returned even if the USPTO does not allow the registration of the trademark. So you can see that it is important to spend extra time making sure that your trademark qualifies for registration before submitting the application. The actual amount of

the filing fee changes from time to time. At the time of writing this book, the filing fee is $335 per class.

The specimen. Although not required at the time of filing an intent-to-use application, ultimately all applications for trademark registration must submit a specimen. The specimen is not the same as the image of the actual trademark itself, but rather shows how the trademark is being used in commerce. For example, for goods, acceptable specimens would include tags, labels, instruction manuals, or containers that show the trademark on the goods or packaging. What are not acceptable specimens for goods? Invoices, announcements, order forms, bills of lading, leaflets, brochures, publicity releases, and other printed advertising materials. For services, acceptable specimens would include signs, photographs, brochures, or advertisements that show the mark used in the sale or advertising of the services.

If the goods or services are classified in more than one international class, you must include specimens that show the mark used on or in connection with at least one item from each class.

Authorized signature. The application must be signed. The appropriate person to sign the application can be the applicant, a person with legal authority to bind the applicant (such as an officer of a corporation if the applicant is a corporation), a person with firsthand knowledge of the facts who has actual or implied authority to act on behalf of the applicant, or an attorney who has an actual or implied written or verbal power of attorney from

the applicant. Together with the signature, the application must identify the position of the signing person (for example, applicant, attorney, vice-president, and so on) and the date of signature.

The Use-Based Application

We have covered the general requirements for all types of trademark applications. Now let's take a look at the specific requirements for the various types of applications. The first application we will look at is the use-based application.

A use-based application is filed when you are currently using the trademark. At the time of filing a use-based application, you are required to submit a specimen indicating how the mark is being used.

In addition, a use-based application must identify two important dates:

- The date the trademark was first used anywhere
- The date the trademark was first used in commerce

The requirement for both of these dates can be a little confusing. The purpose of having both dates is to distinguish between a use that qualifies a user of the mark as obtaining ownership in the mark, and uses that qualify for federal registration. The important date is the use in commerce. The date that the trademark was first used anywhere is the date on which you first used the mark. This could

be an internal use for your company, a use outside of the United States, or a use by another entity on your behalf. The date that the trademark was first used in commerce establishes the date that qualifies you for federal registration.

The first use in commerce is the date on which the trademark was used in commerce that can be regulated by the United States Congress. This includes interstate commerce, territorial commerce, or commerce between the United States and another country. The date of first use anywhere is always either earlier than or equal to the date of first use in commerce.

The dates provided in the application are interpreted as "at least as early as." Thus, if you do not know the exact date, you can enter a date that you know to be correct.

When filing a use-based application, you are required to provide a statement verifying your use of the trademark in commerce.

The Intent-to-Use Application

An intent-to-use application is filed when you have not yet begun use of your trademark. The intent-to-use application allows a person with a bona fide intention to use a trademark to file an application and have that application examined by the USPTO to determine if the trademark qualifies for being registered. Thus, the intent-to-use application allows you to protect your trademark during the

developmental stages of a product or before exposure to the public.

In an intent-to-use application, you must provide a statement indicating that you have a bona fide intent to use the trademark in commerce. Because use has not actually occurred at the time of filing an intent-to-use application, you are not required to submit a specimen at the time of filing. However, prior to the trademark's registration, you must submit a statement of use verifying that you have used the trademark in commerce, and specimens indicating how the trademark is being used in commerce.

The date of filing an intent-to-use application is very important because it establishes the date on which your rights begin. Thus, if the trademark is registered, your rights in the use of the trademark begin on the filing date and you can prevent others from using the trademark except under the following conditions:

- The other person actually used the mark prior to your filing date
- The other person previously filed a trademark application in the United States
- The other person has rights based on a foreign trademark application

The Foreign Registration–Based Application

A trademark application can be filed in the United States based on a trademark registration in another

country. In this situation you must include additional information in the application.

In a trademark application based on a foreign registration, you must include all relevant information about the existing foreign registration. This information includes the following items:

- The country in which the trademark is registered
- The foreign registration number
- The date that the trademark was registered
- The expiration date of the foreign registration
- A copy of the foreign registration certificate

It is not absolutely necessary to include a copy of the foreign registration at the time of filing. However, the foreign registration must be in force at the time of filing the U.S. application and the copy of the registration must be provided prior to your trademark being registered. If the certificate of registration is in a foreign language, you must submit a copy of the foreign registration along with an English translation and a signed statement from the translator stating that the translation is correct.

You can also file a U.S. application based on an application that was filed in a foreign country less than six months before the filing in the United States. In this situation, the foreign filing date will serve as the *priority date* for the U.S. application. For filing an application based on a foreign application, you must include the following information:

- The country in which the application was filed

- The serial number of the foreign application, if known

- The date that the foreign application was filed

Legal-Ease

The **priority date** is the date at which your rights in and to a trademark are created. For applications in the United States, the first use in commerce is your priority date. If you file an intent-to-use application, the filing date is your priority date. If you file the U.S. application within six months of filing the foreign application, the foreign application date will serve as your priority date.

Nuts and Bolts of Applying

A trademark application can be filed either by mailing the application or by filing electronically. The USPTO prefers to receive applications filed electronically. You can file your application using the USPTO website.

Are You TEASing Me, Online Registration?

The USPTO has established on online system for filing applications for trademark registration. The system is called the Trademark Electronic

Application System (TEAS) and can be accessed at www.uspto.gov/teas/eTEASpageA.htm.

Upon accessing this Internet address, you are immediately faced with a decision regarding the type of registration that you want. This includes registration on the principle register, registration on the supplemental register, certification mark registration, collective membership mark registration, or collective trademark/service mark registration.

For any type of registration, there is plenty of online help available as you proceed. Once you select the type of registration, you are given the opportunity to either use a form wizard to create your application or open a standard form that can be filled out.

If you select to use the form wizard, you are first requested to enter the basis of your filing. As we have described already, this can include a use-based, an intent-to-use, or a foreign registration-based application.

The wizard will also request you to identify the number of classes in which you want to register the mark, the number of joint applicants or co-owners of the mark, the number of people that will be signing the application, whether an attorney is filing the application, whether a domestic representative is going to be appointed, whether you will be entering any additional statements (such as a disclaimer or translation), and the method of signing the application.

After completing this initial procedure, TEAS builds a form and displays the form for you to fill out.

TEAS allows you to submit electronic copies of the drawing of your trademark and specimens. This is very convenient, especially if your trademark includes colors. If your trademark does not include colors, you should submit a black and white copy of the trademark.

TEAS allows you to make the payment of the filing fee in one of three methods:

- Credit card
- Automatic deposit account
- Electronic funds transfer

The credit card and electronic funds transfer are the most convenient methods. To use the automatic deposit account, it is necessary to establish this account with the USPTO and maintain a minimum balance.

Once you have filled out the form, at the very bottom of the form is a validation button. When you click this button, TEAS goes through your application to determine if there is any incorrect or missing information. If there are any problems with the information you provided, a window will open on your screen to highlight the errors or problems with your application.

Applying by Snail Mail

The traditional method for filing a trademark application is through the mail. The USPTO used to provide forms that could be downloaded from their website and edited. However, in the interest of

promoting online registrations, these forms are no longer available. However, using TEAS, you can create forms that can be printed out and submitted through the mail. In addition, just about any attorney that files trademarks on a regular basis will have a set of forms for filing trademark applications.

When filing an application through the mail, you need to submit three copies of each specimen. You can file the application with only one copy of the specimen and still obtain a filing date. However, prior to registration of the mark, you must submit the additional copies. In addition, you should file the application using Express Mail available through the U.S. Postal Service. When you use Express Mail, the USPTO considers the postmark date as the filing date. Thus, even if it takes several days for your application to reach the USPTO, you have assurance that the day you mailed your application is going to be your filing date.

The Least You Need to Know

- It is very important to provide all the necessary information, and the correct information, when filing a trademark application.
- If you do not file the application correctly, you will not obtain a filing date and you may forfeit the filing fee.
- You can file a trademark application either online or by using the mail.
- You can file a trademark application on your own or have an attorney file one for you.

The Examination and Registration

In This Chapter

- The examination process of a trademark application
- Responding to rejections by the examining attorney
- Appealing a decision of the examining attorney
- Opposing the registration of a trademark
- Obtaining status of an application or registered trademark

It must have been a very exciting moment when you completed the last step in preparing and filing your application for registering a trademark. We wish we could have been there for the champagne toast. However, shortly after the ol' bubbly wears off, you may start to wonder—what next? When will it be registered? How do I find out what is going on with the process? Who can I call to get

the ball rolling? Believe us, we understand! Patience is one thing, but waiting around without knowing what is going on or without knowing what the status is, well we just didn't get that "virtue." To help you out in this time of need, this chapter provides you with the details of the process, and tells you how to find out what is going on with the process.

Before your trademark is registered, if indeed it can be registered, several things have to happen first. In this chapter, we describe the steps that may be performed between the filing of your application and the registration of your trademark. These steps are referred to as the *examination* of your trademark application. You will learn that depending on what happens at the various steps, the process can be rather quick and painless, or it can be drawn out like a root canal without any nitrous oxide. In addition, the process can vary depending on whether you filed a *use-based* application or an *intent-to-use* application.

One of the major issues that you might have to face during the registration process is an opposition. An opposition is when someone else challenges your right to register the trademark. This chapter describes what an opposition is and how you can respond.

Filing Confirmation

The first step in the examination process is the filing confirmation. When the U.S. Patent and

Trademark Office (USPTO) receives your application for registration, the application is reviewed to determine if it is complete. If the application is complete, then you will receive a notification. This is referred to as a filing receipt. If you filed the application yourself, the filing receipt will be sent directly to you. However, if you have used an attorney, the filing receipt will be sent there instead.

If the application is complete, you will receive the filing receipt rather quickly. If you filed for registration by mail, you should receive the receipt within 1 or 2 months. If you filed electronically, you can receive the filing receipt within a matter of hours.

Swing and a Miss—Filing Errors

Suppose your application is not complete, then what? There are two cases that can arise. The first case is if your application does not include the minimum requirements for obtaining a filing date. The minimum requirements were identified in a previous chapter as the "must haves." If your application does not meet the minimum filing requirements, then you will not be qualified to obtain a filing date for the application. As you have already learned, the filing date is very important for a trademark application. If your application does not qualify for obtaining a filing date, you will have to resubmit your application. If anyone used your trademark during the period of time that it takes for you to prepare and file a new application, you could lose some very important rights.

Another case exists when your application is not complete, but you have at least included the minimum requirements. This case generally arises when you include incorrect information in the application. As long as the provision of the corrected information does not expand the scope of the trademark, you can obtain a filing date for an application in this case.

Base Hit—Obtaining a Filing Date

If your application does meet the minimum requirements—or the must haves—then you will receive a filing receipt. The filing receipt serves as a confirmation that you filed a complete trademark application and it identifies the filing date attributed to the application and a serial number. The serial number will include a two-digit number, followed by a slash, followed by a six-digit number. For example, the serial number for one of the authors' trademarks is 78/142010.

The Filing Receipt

If you filed your trademark application electronically, then you will receive the filing receipt through e-mail. If you mailed your trademark application to the USPTO and did not authorize them to communicate with you through e-mail, then you will receive a paper filing receipt through regular mail.

It is important to understand that even after providing you with a filing receipt, the USPTO might

still determine that your application should not have been awarded a filing date. If this happens, the USPTO will return your application to you and your filing fee will be refunded. You then have the opportunity to cure the deficiencies in your application and refile the application.

The filing receipt will also confirm the information provided in your application. You should review this information very carefully to ensure it has been entered correctly. If you determine that the USPTO has made an error in the information, you need to contact them and request correction.

 Just the Facts

Don't jump the gun on filing a preliminary amendment! It takes the USPTO a little while to get your application into its system. Thus, even though you have received a serial number, it may not appear in the USPTO database for at least 15 days after the initial filing. If you attempt to file a preliminary amendment prior to this time it will not be accepted.

Preliminary Amendment

If upon reviewing the filing receipt, you determine that you made an error in the information you entered, you may file a preliminary amendment. You can file the preliminary amendment either through the mail or electronically by visiting the

USPTO website at eteas.uspto.gov/V2.0/pa200/ WIZARD.htm. For instance, if you entered the wrong mailing address, misspelled information, and so on, you can correct this through a preliminary amendment. The examining attorney will determine whether the changes in your preliminary amendment are permissible within the normal course of his or her review of the application.

It is important to know that not all errors can be corrected through a preliminary amendment. For example, suppose you submitted the wrong mark or you incorrectly listed the goods and/or services. If the change in your preliminary amendment would be considered a *material alteration* then the change will not be accepted. Your only choice of action in this case is to refile the application. Unfortunately, you will also have to repay the filing fee.

Legal-Ease

A **material alteration** in an amendment to a trademark application means that the scope of protection requested in the application has changed. For example, if you attempt to change your trademark from "LAVA GROUP—UNEARTHING LATENT VALUE" to simply "LAVA GROUP", this would be considered a material alteration. If you change the description of goods from "handheld electronic versions of board games" to "electronic games," this would also be considered a material alteration.

Checking Under the Hood

After your application has been reviewed for completeness, it enters into an examination process. The examination process is focused on determining if your trademark qualifies for registration in the United States.

The Examining Attorney

The first step of the examination process is assigning the application to an examining attorney. The examining attorney will communicate directly with the applicant, or the applicant's attorney. However, there is a large gap in time between receiving the filing receipt and hearing from the examining attorney. You can expect to wait for a minimum of four months, but usually no more than six months, before you hear from the examining attorney.

The Review of the Application

In general, applications are examined in the order that they are assigned to the examining attorney. Under special circumstances an applicant can request an application to be examined on an accelerated basis. This is accomplished by filing a petition to make the application *special*. An application is granted special status only under very limited circumstances. If the circumstances would apply equally to a larger number of applications, the request will be denied. The most common reasons for granting a petition to make special is when the

applicant may lose significant rights in the mark. This can include a need for registration as a basis for securing foreign registration or if actual or threatened infringement or pending litigation is eminent.

When it is finally your turn, the examining attorney assigned to your trademark application reviews your application to determine if the trademark should be registered. The ideal scenario is for the examining attorney to determine that the trademark can be registered, and that the description is in perfect form. If this is not the case, then the examining attorney and the applicant must work at obtaining a solution. Ultimately, if the examining attorney agrees that the trademark and description of services should be registered, the trademark is published in the *Official Gazette*. But what happens if all does not go so well?

Round One

In general, the examining attorney evaluates whether the description for your goods and/or services is too broad, too vague, or encompasses more than the listed classifications. In addition, the examining attorney reviews the mark to determine if it is descriptive. The examining attorney might conduct a search for other marks to determine if your mark is confusingly similar to the other marks.

If the examining attorney determines that the trademark should not be registered, he or she will send an official communication to the applicant indicating why the trademark cannot be registered. This is

referred to as an *office action*. Typical grounds for refusing registration include:

- The mark is merely descriptive.
- There is a likelihood of confusion between the applicant's mark and a registered mark.
- The description or a portion of the description of goods and/or services are indefinite.
- The mark is a geographic term or surname.

You are given a period of six months to respond to an Office Action. Failing to respond within six months will result in the application being abandoned. In responding to the Office Action, you are required to address each of the points of rejection provided by the examining attorney. For example, if the examining attorney alleges that your mark is confusingly similar to another mark, you need to present an argument or evidence indicating that the mark is not confusingly similar.

If the examining attorney believes your description is too broad, vague, or indefinite, you may be required to change the description of your goods and services. Typically, the examining attorney will give you suggestions on how to modify the description.

You can respond to the Office Action either electronically or by sending a written response in the mail. Again, the preferred mode of communication is through e-mail. After you have prepared and filed a response, the ball is back in the court of the examining attorney.

Round Two

In the second round of the examination process, one of several actions may occur.

If the examining attorney believes your arguments are persuasive and the examining attorney does not have any additional reasons to refuse your registration, the mark will be published for opposition. This is good news.

However, if the examining attorney identifies additional reasons for refusing registration, he or she may mail another Office Action. If this happens, you are basically back in the same situation that you were in during round one—you have six months to review and respond to the Office Action. This process can go on for many rounds. However, the examining attorneys typically try to limit the examination to no more than two Office Actions.

If the examining attorney does not find your arguments to be persuasive or if your amendments are not accepted, the examining attorney can issue an Office Action with a final refusal. A final refusal can only be issued if all the reasons listed in the Office Action as the basis for refusing registration were presented in an earlier Office Action.

If the examining attorney issues a final refusal for your registration, you are limited on the actions you can take. Similar to any other Office Action, you must respond within six months. Typically, you must respond to a final refusal in one of the following four manners:

- **Request reconsideration.** The applicant may request the examining attorney to reconsider the grounds for refusing registration. Filing a request for consideration gives you the opportunity to convince the examining attorney to remove the refusal; however, the six-month clock continues to run. Thus, if the examiner does not buy into your request for reconsideration, you must take one of the remaining three actions before the six-month period expires to avoid abandonment of your application.

- **Compliance.** If the examining attorney has provided you with modifications to the description of goods or services, or other amendments, in a final refusal, you can agree to comply with the examining attorney's requirements. Typical requirements from the examining attorney include rephrasing of the description of goods and services, disclaiming portions of the mark, and the addition of limiting language in the description.

- **Appeal.** If the examining attorney has refused to register your trademark, you can file an appeal with the Trademark Trial and Appeal Board (TTAB).

- **Petition.** Under certain circumstances, you can file a petition with the director of the USPTO.

> **Just the Facts** _____
>
> The Trademark Trial and Appeal Board hears and decides adversary proceedings involving: oppositions to the registration of trademarks, petitions to cancel trademark registrations, and proceedings involving applications for concurrent use registrations of trademarks. The Board also decides appeals taken from the trademark examining attorneys' refusals to allow registration of trademarks.

The Big Boss–The Trademark Trial and Appeals Board

If your application is refused by the examiner, you can file an appeal with the TTAB. The TTAB is an administrative forum within the USPTO that has the power to make decisions regarding the registration of a mark. The TTAB cannot decide broader issues such as the right to use a mark, or if a mark is being infringed. Although the TTAB is authorized to handle oppositions, concurrent registrations, interferences, and *ex parte* appeals, in round two we will only focus on the *ex parte* appeals function of the TTAB.

If you receive a final refusal, you can contest the decision based on a matter of substance by filing an appeal to the Trademark Trial and Appeal Board.

You can also file an appeal if each of the issues raised by the examining attorney were raised in a previous Office Action.

 Legal-Ease

> *Ex parte* means that the parties are not directly involved in the process but rather, only submit papers and briefs that get reviewed by the TTAB.

The appeal must be filed properly to be effective. The requirements for filing an appeal include:

- **Timing.** The appeal must be filed within six months of the mailing of the final refusal or the Office Action from which the appeal is being made.

- **Payment of fee.** The appeal must be accompanied by the required fee. The fee can change from time to time, so you should check with the USPTO prior to filing your appeal to verify the current fee. At the time of writing this book, the fee for filing an appeal is $100 per class.

- **Compliance with nonappealed issues.** Any issues that were raised by the examining attorney and that are not the subject of the appeal should be complied with prior to filing the appeal.

The appeal is a simple document that states the applicant request reconsideration from the decision of the examining attorney to not allow registration of the mark. You do not have to give any specific reasons for the appeal. One copy of the appeal should be filed and the appeal should include the following information:

- The wording "IN THE UNITED STATES PATENT AND TRADEMARK OFFICE BEFORE THE TRADEMARK TRIAL AND APPEAL BOARD" should appear at the top of the page
- The applicant's name
- The serial number
- The filing date of the application
- The mark involved

The TTAB also decides matters of opposition, interference, and concurrent use. We cover the topic of opposition later in this chapter but we briefly touch on the other two matters here. An interference occurs when two or more applicants have conflicting applications for registration. A proceeding to resolve an interference is declared by the USPTO in response to a person filing a petition with the USPTO. The petition must show that the person would be unduly prejudiced if the interference proceeding did not occur.

A concurrent use proceeding occurs when one or more parties are entitled to a concurrent registration. The TTAB determines concurrent

registration is appropriate and the particular conditions and limitations as to the mode or place of use of the applicant's mark or the goods or services on or in connection with which the mark is used. A concurrent use proceeding is initiated only by filing an application for registration as a lawful concurrent user.

The Petition to the Director

Rather than filing an appeal to the TTAB, you may be allowed to file a petition to the director. A petition to the director should be filed rather than an appeal to the TTAB when the issue in dispute is based on the applicant's compliance (or lack thereof) with a technical provision of the Trademark Act or Trademark Rules of Practice.

A petition cannot be used to challenge substantive issues that arise during examination—these can only be reviewed by the TTAB. Examples of issues that can be addressed through a petition to the director include:

- Whether a disclaimer was properly printed in standardized format.

- Whether an examining attorney acted properly in suspending an application.

- Whether an examining attorney acted properly in holding an application abandoned for failure to file a complete response to an Office Action.

- Whether it was premature for an examining attorney to issue a final action.

Some issues can be handled using either an appeal or a petition to the director. One such example is a requirement for amendment of an identification of goods. However, if you chose to handle an issue through the petition process, you cannot later file an appeal for that same issue.

A petition to the director should include the following information:

- A statement of the relevant facts
- An indication of the points to be reviewed
- A requested action for relief or a remedy
- A filing fee ($100 per class at time of writing this book)

Opposing a Registration

Okay, so you made it through rounds one and two. What happens next? Well, so far the battle to register your trademark has been you against the examiner—and maybe the TTAB also. During this process, the USPTO has agreed that your trademark can be registered so that battle is won. But now the USPTO publishes your trademark in the *Official Gazette* so that the entire world can be put on notice that you have requested registration of your mark. If someone believes that they will be harmed by allowing the registration of your mark, they can file an opposition.

An opposition is filed by a party that wants to prevent a mark from being registered on the Principal Register. Can anyone file an opposition against your registration? Any person who believes that he or she would be damaged by the registration of a mark may file an opposition.

To oppose a registration, a person must file the opposition during the 30 days following the publication date. The opposition must be filed with the TTAB and must state the basis for the opposition (for instance, why the opposing party would be harmed by the registration of the mark).

Rather than filing an opposition, a person may file a request for an extension of time to file an opposition. The request for an extension of time must be filed within the 30-day period after publication. A first 30-day extension of time will be granted simply by filing the request. Further extensions of time may be allowed if there is good cause. Extensions of time beyond 120 days from publication will not be granted unless one of the following conditions is met:

- The applicant signs a consent for the extension.

- The opposing party files a written request stating that the applicant has consented to the request.

- A showing of extraordinary circumstances, assuming that the opposing party could file a petition for cancellation if an opposition was not allowed.

If no oppositions are filed during the 30-day period following publication, the examining attorney will grant registration of the mark.

If an opposition is filed, the applicant and the opposing party enter into an *ex parte* proceeding in which each party must submit evidence in support of their position and the TTAB makes the final decision.

Petition for Cancellation

Now that you have a registered trademark, are you totally out of the woods yet? Well, we hate to give you the bad news but no, someone can still challenge your trademark registration even after you have successfully passed through both rounds of the examination and also the opposition stages. What next? A person can file a petition to cancel your registration.

A cancellation is started when a person files a petition for cancellation, along with the required fee. Similar to an opposition, a petition for cancellation can be filed by any person who believes he or she will be damaged by the continued registration of the mark.

The petition for cancellation may be filed at any time against marks on the supplemental register or within five years from the date of registration for marks on the principle register.

The fee for filing a petition for cancellation can vary over time; at the time of writing this book, the fee is $300 per class.

Checking In—What Is the Status?

The USPTO has made life easy for those of us
who must know the current status. You can determine the status of your application for registration
using one of at least two simple techniques.

- **Online.** You can determine the status of
  a trademark application online at tarr.uspto.
  gov. At this website you can enter search
  criteria based on the U.S. Serial Number,
  the U.S. Registration Number, the USPTO
  Control Number, or the International
  Registration Number.

- **Telephone.** You can call the USPTO to
  determine the status of an application for
  registration. The status telephone number
  is 703-305-8747. Prior to calling the
  status line, you should obtain the U.S. Serial
  Number, the U.S. Registration Number,
  the USPTO Control Number, or the
  International Registration Number.

If you don't know any of the identification numbers
for a trademark application or registered trademark, you can easily determine the numbers by
visiting the USPTO site at www.uspto.gov, selecting the Trademark Search option, and then searching for the mark of interest.

The Least You Need to Know

- During the examination of a trademark application, you must take actions within certain time constraints; if you miss a deadline your application may be abandoned.

- If the examiner continues to reject your registration, you can either file an appeal to the TTAB or a petition to the director.

- After the USPTO has determined that your mark can be registered, it is published for 30 days to allow others to challenge the registration.

- Even after a mark is registered, within certain limits a third-party can attempt to have the registration cancelled.

The Life of a Trademark

In This Chapter

- The span of duration for trademark protection
- How the protection of a trademark can be ended
- Duties of a trademark holder
- How a trademark becomes diluted
- How a trademark becomes generic

Do you remember having to take penmanship classes while you were in school? For those of us that live in a world of chicken-scratch writing, this was a very painful experience. Our only salvation was the invention of the computer and word processing.

But picture this setting: We are not sure this is how it happened but at least this is how we envision it. On a hot summer day in Atlanta, Georgia, during the mid-1880s, Dr. John S. Pemberton stops by to visit his bookkeeper Frank Robinson. In Mr. Robinson's wood-paneled office, windows open, an overhead fan gently rotating above, lights off just to keep any

extra heat from being generated, and piles of folders and boxes neatly spread about the room, the two sit across the desk from each other in worn-out leather chairs. The topic of conversation—a new drink that Dr. Pemberton had invented. The drink included extracts of cocaine as well as the caffeine-rich kola nut. Mr. Robinson, who obviously paid attention in his penmanship class, suggested a name for the drink and then neatly scripted the words on a piece of paper. Since doctors are not really known for the penmanship, it is a good thing that Mr. Robinson scripted the name rather than Dr. Pemberton, because today his writing is probably the most world-renowned trademark—Coca-Cola. Can you imagine what chaos the world would be in today had Dr. Pemberton scripted the trademark? The only people that could read the mark would be pharmacists.

On May 14, 1892, a registration for the Coca-Cola trademark was filed in the United States and on January 31, 1893, the mark became a federally registered mark. Today, the Coca-Cola trademark is vigorously marketed and monitored and is still protected under trademark laws in almost every country.

When will the Coca-Cola trademark expire? In this chapter, you will learn about the life span of a trademark before and after it has been registered. You will also learn what is required to renew a trademark registration as well as events that can happen or actions you can take (or not take) that might result in decreasing the value of the trademark or resulting in the loss of trademark protection.

Span of Protection

Obviously time spans have a beginning and an end. Looking at the span of protection for a trademark, we need to identify when a person's rights in a trademark begin, and when the person's rights end. As you will learn, once you obtain rights in a trademark, going forward, the span of protection for the trademark can be forever.

Good Counsel

Don't confuse the ownership of a trademark with the registration of a trademark. You can own a trademark without registering the trademark. However, it is a good idea to register the trademark because it provides constructive nationwide notice.

When Protection Rights Begin

As discussed in Chapter 5, a person's rights in a trademark begin when the person uses that mark in commerce. Thus, when the mark is attached to a product and sold, the rights in the use of that mark begin. There are common law or state law rights associated with trademarks as well as federal law rights. The common law or state law rights are limited in geographic scope. Thus, a user of a trademark obtains rights in the geographic area that the mark is used. When a trademark is registered with the U.S. government, the geographic constraints are basically lifted.

Of course, the ideal scenario is for you to file a federal registration for a mark on or prior to your first use of the mark. Assuming the ideal scenario, your span of protection for your trademarks begins at the time you first use the trademark in commerce and at a minimum, it begins when you file a trademark application.

When Protection Rights End

The good news is that once you acquire rights in a trademark, you can keep those rights indefinitely—as long as you don't abandon the mark or the mark becomes what is known as a *generic mark*. We will address in detail each of the ways in which you can lose protection of a trademark later in this chapter. But for now, the general rule of thumb is that you can maintain protection of a trademark as long as you want to if you meet certain criteria and the following events to do not occur:

- The trademark registration is not renewed
- The trademark is abandoned
- The trademark becomes a generic name
- The trademark is cancelled

The ability to protect a trademark indefinitely is consistent with the purposes of trademark law—to avoid *confusion* as to the origin or source of goods or services. Just imagine if the Coca-Cola trademark was suddenly unable to be protected. The trademark has acquired worldwide familiarity. If others were allowed to put the Coca-Cola trademark onto

their products, they would unfairly reap the benefit of the good will associated with the name, and consumers would be at a total loss as to whether a product was actually a product of the Coca-Cola Company, or a knock-off product.

Legal-Ease

When a trademark becomes **generic**, that means the trademark has become a common name for the goods or services that are associated with it.

The standard for determining **confusion** is whether or not it would be likely for an ordinary consumer to be confused as to the source of goods or services.

The longer a trademark is used, the more popular and recognizable it can become. Obviously, the more popular and recognizable a mark becomes, the mark becomes more powerful and valuable. If the span of protection for a mark was only for a finite period of time, it would cause quite a substantial amount of chaos in the marketplace. The motivation to create strong marks would be greatly diminished due to the fact that others, after a period of time, would be able to use the marks.

Renewals and Fees

You have already learned how to register your trademark, so what's next in the process? Just sit back and

enjoy the domain that you have established in your trademark? No. You actually have some additional things that you have to do to maintain your rights and protect your trademark.

Just the Facts

The Under Secretary of Commerce for Intellectual Property is the director of the U.S. Patent and Trademark Office. The Patent Office as a distinct bureau dates from the year 1802 when a separate official in the Department of State who became known as Superintendent of Patents was placed in charge of patents. In 1975, the name of the Patent Office was changed to the Patent and Trademark Office. When we refer to the director or the director of the Trademark Office, we refer to the appointed director to the U.S. Patent and Trademark Office.

The U.S. code states that once a trademark is registered, the trademark registration will remain in force for a period of 10 years unless you do not file an Affidavit of Continued Use at the end of six years following the registration of the mark. The registration of the mark can be increased indefinitely if you file an Affidavit of Continued Use after each successive 10-year period following the registration of the mark.

The director of the Trademark Office might cancel a registration if the owner of the registration fails to comply with these, and other ongoing requirements.

When Are Trademark Registrations Renewed?

The owner of a trademark registration must renew the registration during the one-year period immediately preceding the end of the current registration. For example, if you registered your trademark on June 24, 1987, you would have been required to renew the registration during the one-year period of time extending from June 25, 1996 to June 24, 1997. Every 10-year period will require an additional application for renewal.

How Is a Trademark Registration Renewed?

To renew a trademark registration, the owner of the registration must file an *affidavit* with the USPTO, along with a required fee. The affidavit filed with the USPTO must include the following elements:

 Legal-Ease

An **affidavit** is a written declaration or statement that is made under oath and before a notary public or authorized officer.

- Identification of the goods or services recited in the original registration or in connection with which the mark is in use in commerce

- Specimens or facsimiles showing current use of the mark

OR

- Identification of the goods or services recited in the original registration or in connection with which the mark is not in use

- Showing that the nonuse of the trademark is due to special circumstances which excuse such nonuse and is not due to any intention to abandon the mark

As discussed in Chapter 5, a trademark can be registered on the principle register or the supplemental register. The rules regarding the renewal of registrations apply to trademarks on both the principle and supplemental registers.

What Is the Cost for Renewing a Trademark Registration?

The cost for renewing a trademark application can vary from year to year and should be checked prior to filing a renewal. At the time of writing this book, the current fee for renewing a trademark registration is $400 per trademark classification. A single trademark might be registered in one or more classifications. Of course, if you use an attorney to prepare and file the application for renewal, there will be additional costs associated with the attorney's fees.

What Happens If You Miss Your Renewal?

If you missed your date for renewing your trademark registration, relax, you might not be totally

out of luck. The U.S. law gives you a grace period
of six months after the end of the one-year time
period to submit an application for renewal. But,
don't think it is *that* easy. To file your application for
renewal during the six-month grace period the government makes you pay for your tardiness. The
fee charged for filing your application for renewal
during the six-month grace period can vary from
year to year so, remember to check prior to filing
your application for renewal. At the time of writing
this book, the current fee for filing the application
during the six-month grace period is $100 per trade-
mark class. Notice that this fee is in addition to the
$400 per trademark class for renewing the mark.

Filing a Deficient Application for Renewal

So you decided not to use an attorney and you filed
your application for renewal all by yourself. A few
weeks later you get a notification from the USPTO
that your application for renewal was deficient.
What do you do now? First of all you need to figure out what was deficient about your initial filing.
Then you need to fix the deficiency and refile
the application for renewal. The notification will
indicate the time period that you have for correcting
the deficiencies in the application. When filing the
corrected application, it is necessary to include an
additional fee. The additional fee can vary from year
to year so you should make sure that you verify the
correct value prior to filing your corrected application. At the time of writing this book, the current
fee for filing the corrected application is $100.

Abandoning Your Mark

One way that you can lose your rights in a trademark registration is to abandon the trademark. This fine if you intend to leave the mark behind, but it can be a very bad thing if you do something, or fail to do something, that qualifies as abandonment if indeed you did not intend to abandon the trademark.

According to the U.S. code, a trademark is deemed to be abandoned if either of the following two conditions occurs:

- Discontinued use of the trademark
- The trademark becomes generic

Discontinued Use of a Trademark

A trademark can become abandoned if the owner of the trademark discontinues use of the trademark without an intent to resume use at a later date. The failure to use a trademark for three consecutive years is considered *prima facie* evidence of abandonment of the trademark. In addition, the intent not to resume use of a trademark can be inferred from the circumstances.

Let's look at an example. Suppose you have obtained a registration for the service mark Lu Lu's Nannies On Call that you have used in connection with a nanny business that you used to pay for your college education. When you graduated from college with a business degree, you entered the corporate world with great vim and vigor. Five years later you decide

that you have had enough with Corporate America, and you return to your true love, the nanny business. Can you revive Lu Lu's Nannies On Call? Yes, you can, provided that in the interim, no other parties have begun use of the service mark or registered the service mark. However, as you will read later in this chapter, you might be prevented from further use of the service mark. This can occur if another party has adopted the service mark and filed a petition to cancel your registration of the service mark.

It is important to note that use of the trademark, as discussed throughout this book, means a bona fide use of the trademark in the ordinary course of trade. Thus, merely using the mark simply for purposes of reserving a right in the trademark is not considered a valid use. For example, in Lu Lu's Nannies On Call example, simply running a periodic advertisement in a local newspaper without actually having intent to provide the services would not qualify as a use.

The Trademark Becomes Generic

When a mark becomes generic, it can completely destroy the owner's trademark rights. We address this issue in more detail later in this chapter, but for now you need to know that a trademark is generic when the general populace associates the trademark as the actual name of the product. For example, when you hear the word *escalator* you do not think of it as a trademark, you basically associate it with moving steps just the way you associate the word ladder with a ladder and door with a door. However, when the escalator was first invented, the word escalator was used as a trademark. Today, it is a generic term.

So if the owner of a trademark engages in any conduct that results in the trademark becoming a generic name for the goods or services associated with the trademark, the trademark can become abandoned. It is also important to note that the trademark can become abandoned if the owner fails to take actions and such inaction results in a trademark becoming generic.

Cancellation of Registration

As you have read earlier in this book, when an application to register a trademark is filed, the trademark is published in the *Official Gazette*. The publication of the trademark affords others the opportunity to oppose registration of the trademark based on various reasons. Well, once a trademark is registered on the Principle Register, other parties can still challenge the registration of the trademark. The process of challenging a trademark registration on the Principle Register is referred to as a *cancellation*.

Who Can Cancel a Registration?

A trademark registration can only be cancelled by the USPTO. However, the cancellation of a trademark registration can be initiated by the two following entities or groups of parties:

- Anyone who believes they will be damaged as a result of the registration of the trademark on the Principle Register
- The Federal Trade Commission

A person who wants to cancel a trademark registration must believe that they will be damaged by the registration. This damage can include dilution that would occur based on the registration of the trademark. Let's look at an example.

Suppose that you started to use a trademark in connection with selling a large plastic ring under the name of Hula-Hoop. Your product is a hit and becomes the rage of the teenage crowd. Shortly thereafter, Sneaky Inc. seeks to register the mark Hula-Hoop in connection with toys for children. Obviously, you and your business can be greatly damaged by such registration. How can you be damaged? Well, it is very likely that the general public would think that the toys being sold under the mark Hula-Hoop are associated with your product. Thus, Sneaky Inc. could gain popularity and obtain sales based on the fame associated with your mark. This is considered damage.

How a Trademark Registration Is Cancelled

A trademark registration might be cancelled when a person, believing that he or she will be damaged by the registration of the trademark on the principle register, files a petition to cancel the registration.

There is a cost associated with canceling a trademark. To file a petition for cancellation, the person filing the petition must pay a fee. The value of the fee can vary from year to year, but at the time of writing this book, the fee for filing a petition to cancel a trademark registration is $300 for each class that the trademark is registered.

The petition to cancel a trademark registration must be filed within five years from the date that the mark was registered on the Principle Register. However, a trademark can be cancelled at any time under the following conditions:

- The trademark becomes generic.
- The trademark is functional.
- The trademark has been abandoned.
- The registration was obtained fraudulently.

If a trademark becomes a generic name for the goods or services, or a portion of the goods or services for which it is registered, then an eligible party can file for cancellation of the registration. If the trademark is generic for only a portion of the goods or services, then the cancellation will only be effective as to that portion of the registration.

It should be noted that a registered trademark is not deemed to be the generic name of a product simply because the trademark is also used as a name for a unique product or service. The test for determining if a trademark has become generic is the primary significance of the trademark to the relevant public in comparison to the significance of the trademark as a motivation to purchase. In short, when you hear the word "aspirin" you think of headache relief, not a branded product. Aspirin is a generic name.

Cancellation of Certification Marks

Any eligible person might file a petition to cancel a certification trademark at any time under the following grounds:

- The registrant of the trademark does not control, or is not able to legitimately exercise control over, the use of the mark.

- The registrant engages in the production or marketing of any goods or services to which the certification mark is applied.

- The registrant permits the use of the trademark for purposes other than for certification.

- The registrant discriminately refuses to certify or to continue to certify the goods or services of any person who maintains the standards or conditions that the trademark certifies.

Generic Marks

As previously discussed, the registration of a trademark can be cancelled, and you can lose your ownership in a trademark if the trademark becomes generic. This is a very serious problem in the world of trademarks and many companies spend millions of dollars to prevent their trademarks from becoming generic.

We have already mentioned the trademark *escalator*, which has certainly become a generic name. There

are many more examples of such marks. A few trademarks that have become generic include:

- Allen wrench
- aspirin
- cellophane
- cola
- granola
- jungle gym
- linoleum
- tarmac
- yo-yo
- zipper

A trademark owner has to take active steps to prevent a trademark from becoming generic. A trademark owner should never use a mark as a noun or a verb, because such actions imply that the trademark is generic. For example, the owner of the mark escalator should not have allowed uses of the mark such as "take the escalator to the second floor" or "don't take the steps, take the escalator."

Proper use of a trademark is to use it as a *branding name* not a noun or verb. For example, it would be proper to state "take the Escalator brand mode of transportation to the second floor." You can see that such uses can be somewhat awkward. However, you have to be clever and careful in your use of the trademark or you might find yourself without one.

Xerox

When your trademark is commonly used by consumers, you have to take special proactive measures to prevent it from becoming generic. Xerox is an example of a trademark that came very close to passing into the world of generic marks, but due

to a massive and expensive advertising campaign, it was just barely saved. It was becoming very commonplace to ask someone to make a Xerox of a document. To avoid their mark from becoming generic, the Xerox Corporation took out ads advising consumers to "photocopy" instead of "Xeroxing" documents. Thus, it was appropriate to say, "make a Xerox photocopy of a document" but it was not appropriate to say "make a Xerox of this document."

BAND-AID

Johnson & Johnson had a close call with their BAND-AID trademark used to describe adhesive bandages. The Johnson & Johnson jingle of "I am stuck on BAND-AIDS, 'cause BAND-AID's stuck on me" had to be rewritten. Johnson & Johnson took the path of identifying BAND-AID as a brand name by modifying their jingle to be "I am stuck on BAND-AID brand, 'cause BAND-AID's stuck on me."

Dilution of a Trademark

Dilution of a trademark occurs when the capacity of a famous mark to identify goods or services is diminished. The owner of a trademark has an ongoing obligation to police the use of the trademark and prevent dilution. The owner of a trademark has the right to prevent uses of marks that can cause dilution of a trademark. This right is available regardless of whether or not the potentially diluting use is being conducted by a competitor or whether

the use results in a likelihood of confusion, mistake, or deception. An example of dilution would be advertising for Nike guitars. The owner of the Nike trademark should request a party using the company's mark in this manner to stop.

If a trademark becomes diluted, the term of protection of the trademark can be ended. If only portions of the goods or services that the trademark is used to identify are diluted, then the term of protection of the trademark with respect to the portion of goods or services can be ended.

The Least You Need to Know

- The protection of a trademark can last forever if the owner of the trademark continues to use the trademark and does not do anything to forfeit ownership in the trademark.

- The duration of protection for a trademark can be cut short if the trademark registration is not renewed, if the trademark is abandoned, if the trademark is cancelled, or if the trademark becomes a generic name.

- The owner of a trademark registration has an ongoing duty to police the use of the trademark and ensure that the mark is not becoming diluted or being used as a generic term.

- Even after a trademark has been registered, another party can seek to have the trademark cancelled if they are damaged by the registration of the mark.

Domain Names and Trademarks

In This Chapter

- Understanding the difference between domain names and trademarks
- Your ability to trademark a domain name
- Domain name disputes and resolutions

By this time, you may have heard the terms *domain* and *domain name extension*, but what exactly are they? A domain is a website address, complete with an extension, which is the ending on a website address. These extensions include the popular *.com*, *.net*, *.org*, and *.edu* but also less popular ones like *.biz*, *.info* and *.ws* (among others).

Companies typically reserve domains that reflect their business in some way, whether that's the actual name of the business (like www.lavagroup.net, reflecting our company's name, LAVA Group), or the business that you're in (such as www.handyman.com, which could reflect the type of work you do).

In terms of extensions, they are also known as top-level domain name extensions. These domain name extensions help direct the traffic over the internet and are also supposed to provide you with some information about the company (for example, .org is supposed to be for organizations and associations, while .com is supposed to be for commercial entities).

www.notatrademark.com

You should know that domain names are not trademarks. Rather, they're merely your address on the web. As such, they don't convey any specific authority to you (other than your ownership of the domain), but may serve to establish that you're using or promoting your services in the marketplace. Therefore, it may be worthwhile to obtain additional protection on your domain name, such as a trademark, if protection is available.

Can a Domain Name Be Registered as a Trademark?

So should you federally register your domain name as a mark? Can you federally register your domain name as a mark?

Let's look at an example. Say your company name is LAVA Group and you're a firm helping companies manage and make money off of their intellectual property. You may have registered LAVA

Group as a service mark federally. You may also reserve the domain name www.ipcommercialization. com, because you know that customers looking to make money off of their intellectual property may simply type in www.ipcommercialization.com to learn more about these types of services. But can you federally register www.ipcommercialization.com as a service mark?

The USPTO looks at registration of a domain name just as they look at registration of any other mark—it has to meet the criteria for registration. What does that mean? The mark, in its entirety, must identify the goods and services you offer, it must be distinctive and it must serve as a source indicating function (who is providing the services). Going back to our example, clearly the www and the .com don't serve a source indicating function— millions of companies out there have the identical indicators. Therefore, sticking www and .com onto ipcommercialization doesn't make the domain name a valid service mark.

As a result, an applicant must rely on the non-identifier portions of the mark to gain registration. In our example, that's ipcommercialization. However, earlier we said that we think most people looking for these types of services would stick that into their web browsers. That means we think it's descriptive! If it's descriptive, then it's not distinctive and can't be registered.

Internet Corporation for Assigned Names and Numbers

So who controls domain names? The Internet Corporation for Assigned Names and Numbers (ICANN) is responsible for managing and coordinating the issuance of domain names. It was necessary to vest this authority in one organization to ensure that the same domain name is not issued to two different people. This system also ensures when you type in a domain name, you're directed properly to the appropriate website.

ICANN coordinates the issuance of domain names by authorizing specific companies to field consumers' purchase requests for domain names. These requests are routed and coordinated through ICANN to ensure there is no duplication. The companies that have the authority to issue domain names are called *registrars*.

How Can I Register a Domain Name?

If you want to register a domain name, there's a variety of companies that are authorized by ICANN to issue top-level domains. We've included a list of some of these companies in our online resource list in Chapter 12. Domain names may be registered for variable periods ranging from a year to several years.

Cybersquatting

In the mid- to late 1990s, clever but somewhat unethical individuals took advantage of many companies' failure to obtain the domain names for their registered trademarks. These individuals registered a large number of famous trademarks as domain names for no other reason than to hold the trademark owners ransom for large payments to get the domain names back. This activity is called *cybersquatting*. For example, Panasonic, Hertz, and Avon were all victims of cybersquatting.

Legal-Ease

Cybersquatting is the bad-faith registration of a domain for profit.

Why was cybersquatting so effective? Many individuals simply put a company's name between *www* and *.com* and assumed that it is a website connected with the company. As a result, consumers looking for a particular company end up at an erroneous website or a page that indicates that no website is available.

Just the Facts

Did you know that certain domain names are worth a lot of money? In 1999, eCompanies purchased *www.business.com* for $7.5 million. It's no wonder cybersquatters have popped up.

The Anticybersquatting Consumer Protection Act

If you have been the victim of cybersquatting, there is action that you can take. In 1999, the United States Congress adopted the Anticybersquatting Consumer Protection Act (ACPA). This act authorized trademark owners to sue cybersquatters and force them to transfer the domain name back to the owner. In certain circumstances, the company can also receive money damages from the cybersquatter.

However, certain steps must be taken to prove an individual has committed cybersquatting:

- The domain name registrant had a bad-faith intent to profit from the trademark.
- The trademark was distinctive at the time the domain name was first registered.
- The domain name is identical or confusingly similar to the trademark.
- The trademark qualifies for protection under federal trademark laws (the mark is distinctive and was first used in commerce by the owner).

You'll note that the intent of the individual accused of cybersquatting is important. Therefore, if the alleged cybersquatter can show that he or she had a real reason (other than to extract money!) to register the name, then the person will be off the hook (and be able to keep the domain name).

Objections

Cybersquatting is a serious offense with fines up to $100,000 per domain name offense!

Derogatory Domain Names and Websites

Is it cybersquatting or trademark infringement to register and operate the website www.cokestinks. com or to run a site blasting a company, while using their trademark? Many individuals have obtained disparaging domain names and operated sites re-lated to products or services that they dislike. The most famous example of this involved an angered customer of Bally's Total Fitness, the health club. The member claimed that he had tried to cancel his membership to the club, but Bally's ended up charg-ing him the entire membership fee *again*. So what's an angered customer to do? Launch Bally's Total Fitness Sucks. Seems like a slam dunk to shut these sites down, right? Not exactly. You may recall our earlier discussion of parody in Chapter 3. Is there really a likelihood that a consumer would think Bally's launched this website? Of course, no com-pany in their right mind would operate a website blasting their own services! As a result, the courts rejected Bally's argument and the site lived on.

> **Good Counsel**
>
> If you're at all concerned that your company could be the target of these types of attacks, then you should register derogatory variations of your trademarks as domain names (to preclude others from doing so). You can just register the names and not bother putting up a site. Then, if anyone types in www.yourcompanystinks.com, they'll receive either Under Construction or an error such as *page not found*.

Domain Name Disputes

So what happens if someone has registered and is using a domain name that you believe rightfully belongs to you? ICANN has developed a domain name dispute policy that outlines the circumstances under which you can challenge this registration and use. (You can review the policy at www.icann.org/dndr/udrp/policy.htm.) This policy has been adopted by all registrars. We are now going to outline the key aspects of this policy, as well as the requirements for you to prevail in asserting inappropriate ownership by someone else.

Your Representations

When you register for a domain name, the registrar requires that you agree to a registration agreement. In that agreement, you agree that (a) the statements

that you make when registering your domain name
are complete and accurate (including the contact
and address information); (b) to your knowledge, the
registration of the domain name will not infringe
upon or otherwise violate the rights of any third
party (this means that you're not registering someone else's valid trademark); you are not registering
the domain name for an unlawful purpose; and you
will not knowingly use the domain name in violation
of any applicable laws or regulations.

When Domain Names Will Be Transferred

In the case of a dispute, the registrar will cancel
or transfer a domain name registration based on a
court order or the registrar's receipt of a decision
from an administrative panel requiring the cancellation or transfer.

What Do You Have to Assert?

For you to prevail in a domain name dispute, you
have to assert and prove each of the following items:

- The domain name is identical or confusingly
  similar to a trademark or service mark in
  which you have rights.

- The person who registered the domain name
  has no legitimate interest or rights in the
  domain name.

- The domain name has been registered and
  is being used in bad faith.

How Do You Prove It?

ICANN has outlined some specific ways that you can prove each of the above factors. These are just suggested approaches as there may be other evidence that can also prove your case. They include evidence indicating:

- The person registered the domain name for the purpose of making money off it in excess of how much the purchaser paid for it. Examples might include a person's attempts to sell the domain name to the rightful owner or a competitor of the rightful owner.

- The person registered the domain name to stop the trademark owner from obtaining a domain name with the trademark included in it.

- The person registered the domain name to disrupt the business of a competitor.

- The person registered the domain name to attract customers intending to go to the trademark owner's website (truly creating a likelihood of confusion).

If You're on the Receiving End of a Complaint ...

Innocent until proven guilty, right? Don't assume all instances of domain name disputes involve a rightful trademark owner and a scoundrel cybersquatter. You may be on the receiving end of a complaint. So how should you respond? Here are a few examples of how you can prove your rightful ownership of a domain name:

- Before learning of the dispute, you were either offering or intended to offer goods or services that corresponded to the domain name.

- You or your company are generally known by the domain name, even if you never obtained any service or trademark rights.

- You're not intending to use the domain name to profit or to confuse consumers, but rather you've commenced or intend to commence a real, noncommercial, or fair use of the domain name.

The Procedure for Filing a Complaint

ICANN has created an entire set of rules of procedure related to filing and responding to a domain name dispute. It contains everything you need to know regardless of the side of the dispute you are on. These procedures and information include:

- What should be contained in the complaint
- Who to file the complaint with
- How to give notice to the other side
- Costs and expenses
- How to respond to a complaint

To review the procedures, you can go to the ICANN website at www.icann.org/dndr/udrp/uniform-rules.htm.

Domain Names and Famous People

Famous people's names are not trademarked, right? Wrong! Famous individuals may not federally register their names, but you must remember that they enjoy common law rights to their names in the geographic areas in which they're used (and for famous folks, that's just about everywhere). That means that stars can rely on the same procedures outlined above.

Who Owns a Domain Name?

As you can see, it is often useful to find out the name of the owner of a particular domain name and, perhaps, when the domain name is set to expire. This information can be obtained at www. whois.net. However, please note that sometimes the person registering a particular mark can request (for an additional charge) anonymity.

The Least You Need to Know

- It may make sense to register your domain name as a trademark.
- You must clear the same hurdles for registration of a domain name as any other trademark.
- There are dispute resolution procedures available to you if your trademark is registered as a domain name by someone else.

Do You Own Your Trademark?

In This Chapter

- What is required to own a trademark?
- Can you file an application if you don't own the mark?
- How to expand your ownership rights in a trademark
- How is the ownership in a trademark assigned to others?

You may be an owner and not even know it. How could that be? Suppose you own your own business. If your business provides services to others, then the name of your company is most likely a service mark and since you own the business you also own the service mark. If your business sells products to others and you attach a product name to that product then once again, you own a trademark. A name that is attached to a product to identify the source of that product is a trademark and once again, since you own the company, you own the trademark.

As you can see, it is relatively easy to gain ownership in a trademark if you own a business. However, the extent of your ownership can vary greatly depending on how you use your trademark and whether you register your trademark with the federal government.

In this chapter, we describe how ownership rights are created in a trademark and how you can expand those rights or, if you are not careful, how further expansion of your rights can be limited. In addition, we describe how ownership of a trademark can be acquired or given to someone else through the use of an assignment.

Use It and It's Yours

What are the requirements for owning a trademark? You are the owner of a trademark if you meet one of the following requirements:

- You have to be the first to use mark in commerce.
- You acquired the mark through an assignment from the previous owner.

You have also learned that a trademark can be registered with the federal government. Can you own a trademark that is not registered with the federal government? Certainly. The previously listed requirements for owning a trademark do not make any mention of a requirement to register the trademark with the federal government.

When you use a trademark for providing goods or services, you become the owner of that trademark. However, your ownership is limited to the geographic regions in which you have used or are using the trademark. For example, you may open a fast food restaurant in Bowling Green, Kentucky, to make and serve a special fried chicken recipe. Let's say you call your restaurant Kentucky Fried Chicken. The moment you begin providing services with that mark, you become the owner of the mark. However, if another person begins to use the same mark in a different location, then that person will also obtain ownership rights in the mark.

Can you obtain ownership of a trademark based on the use by someone else? Yes, you can obtain ownership in a trademark if the use of that trademark *inures* to your benefit. Thus, you can establish ownership in a trademark that is being used by an entity. To do so, you should have an agreement in place that indicates that the entities use of the trademark inures to your benefit. For example, you may hire a marketing company to promote your business or product. In performing this task, the marketing company might use certain marks. Your agreement with the marketing company should ensure that you are the owner of any marks used in the promotion of your business or products.

You can also obtain ownership of a trademark through an assignment. For example, if you purchase a business from someone else, you want to obtain ownership in the trademarks associated with the business. This is accomplished through an assignment agreement.

Just the Facts _____

Inures is a legal term. In the context of using a trademark, the statement that "a use inures to your benefit" means that the use is attributed to you as though you were the one actually using the trademark.

Good Counsel _____

When you are purchasing a business from someone else, it is very important to make sure that you wrap up the intellectual property rights—including trademark ownership. Make sure that the agreement provides you with all rights in and to the trademark and the goodwill associated with the trademark.

Expansion of Ownership

You can expand the ownership of your trademark. This can be accomplished by further use of the trademark or through registering the trademark.

Expansion Through Use

Whenever you are the first to use a trademark in a territory, under common law you gain rights to that trademark in that territory. Thus, although the initial ownership in a trademark may be limited

to a very small geographic region, as your business expands into other territories, your ownership in the trademark may also expand.

Expansion Through Registration

You can quickly expand your ownership rights nationwide through registering your trademark with the U.S. Patent and Trademark Office (USPTO). Registering a trademark with the USPTO, among other things, serves as nationwide notice and gives you nationwide priority. This is a huge benefit because it immediately expands your area of protection to a broader geographic region.

If you do not register your trademark with the USPTO, the geographic footprint of your ownership is limited to the areas in which you have used the trademark. This is not a serious problem for a large company that is already operating nationwide. For instance, assume Parker Brothers introduced a new board game to the market or Columbia Pictures comes out with a new movie. Both of these events pretty much have instantaneous nationwide impact. Thus, the trademarks associated with the board game or movie would obtain nationwide coverage under common law.

However, if you are Scooter's Unicycle Service, Inc., mainly providing unicycle repair services in a limited number of cities, the trademarks and service marks associated with your business will only be protected in the areas in which you operate. Without federal registration, every time you expand your business

into a new territory, you expand your area of ownership, but only if someone else in that territory has not already used the trademark. Thus, if you plan to expand your company or the territories in which you provide products or services, registering your trademarks with the USPTO is not only wise but a good business investment.

Slamming the Door on Expansion

Similar to your ability to expand instantly the ownership of your mark nationwide through federal registration, your competitors can do the same thing. If someone else is using the same or similar trademark as yours, they can file for federal registration with the USPTO. If their trademark is registered, then you can be prevented from further expansion of your use of the trademark. Yikes!

Yours or Your Employer's Trademark

Suppose you are working for a company and you think of a new product name or a new name under which to market the services of the company—do you own that trademark? The answer is no. First of all, just thinking of a trademark to use does not establish any ownership rights; you have to actually use the trademark to create ownership rights.

Can you file a trademark application to register a trademark you thought of and then sell it to your company, or for that matter, any other company? The answer again is no. You can only file an application for registration of a trademark if you are

actually using the trademark or have a bona fide intent to use the trademark. If you simply want to register a trademark that you will later sell, you do not have any ownership in the trademark and thus cannot file for registration. What about filing an intent-to-use application and then selling that to your company? Nope, the government thought of that also. Any attempt to assign or sell rights of a trademark that is the subject of an intent-to-use trademark application will be void.

Who Can Own a Trademark?

Ownership of trademark can rest with a single entity or by more than one person or entity.

Single Entity Ownership

Generally, a trademark is owned by a single entity; however, that entity can take on several forms. When applying for registration of a trademark, the entity needs to be identified in the application. The following entities may own and apply for registration of a trademark:

- Individual
- Corporation
- Partnership
- Limited partnership
- Joint venture
- Sole proprietorship
- Trust
- Estate

It is important to determine who is the owner of a trademark prior to filing an application to register federally the trademark. An application to register a

trademark must be filed by the owner of the mark. In the case of an intent-to-use application, the application must be filed by a person who is entitled to use the mark in commerce. If an application for registration is filed by someone other than the owner of the trademark, the application is void and it cannot be amended to identify the correct party.

Just the Facts

The United States is one of the very few countries in the world that require use before registering a trademark. Other countries include Canada and the Philippines.

Joint Ownership

In some cases, a trademark may be owned by more than one person or entity. It is important to determine whether this case applies to your trademark. Normally, a trademark application is filed in the name of a single party—an individual, company, partnership, and so on. However, if two or more parties are involved in the use of a trademark, the mark can be jointly owned. If you list multiple parties when filing a trademark application, the USPTO will presume that the trademark and the business in which it is used are actually owned by separate parties jointly and cannot be identified correctly in any other way.

Take the following example: In the interest of the Atkins Diet, Kentucky Fried Chicken and

Coca-Cola decide to pool their research and development teams to come up with a new product— liquid carbonated meat. Further, suppose the two companies agree to market the beverage under the name of Chica-Cola. If the two companies do not create a joint venture to develop and market the product, but instead maintain individual status with relationship to the product, then they can file a trademark application as joint owners.

If a trademark is jointly owned, then the application must include all relevant information for each of the applicants, and each of the applicants must sign the application, since they are individual parties and not a single entity.

Good Counsel

If a trademark is jointly owned, absent an agreement between the parties, each owner is free to license and assign his portion of the ownership. This could be detrimental if a portion of the ownership is assigned to a competitor. You should be very careful when deciding if your mark should be jointly owned.

Changing Ownership of a Trademark

Can you assign your ownership in a trademark to someone else? Yes, any registered trademark, or any trademark for which an application for registration has been filed, can be assigned.

Assignment Requirements

An assignment of ownership in a trademark must be in a written agreement and it must be signed by the owner assigning the trademark. Thus, an assignment of a trademark cannot be performed as an oral agreement.

What Gets Assigned?

When you assign your ownership in a trademark, the receiving party gets the right to use the trademark. In addition, the receiving party obtains the goodwill in the business in which the trademark is used. If the trademark is only associated with a portion of the business, then that portion of the goodwill connected with the use of the trademark is included.

Assignment of an Intent-to-Use Application

You cannot assign ownership of an intent-to-use trademark application. In order to assign your ownership in an intent-to-use application, you must first file a statement of use. The reason ownership in an intent-to-use trademark cannot be assigned is because there is no goodwill associated with the trademark.

Recordation of Assignment

Any assignment of a trademark should be recorded in the U.S. Patent and Trademark Office. The failure to record an assignment can be detrimental to

the person or company receiving the mark. If an assignment is not recorded within three months of being signed, then the assignment will be void provided that anyone else purchases the ownership of the trademark or is assigned the ownership of the trademark for valuable consideration, and they have not received notice of the previous assignment.

To record an assignment, the assignment must be filed with the U.S. Patent and Trademark Office. The assignment is basically a contract or agreement that typically identifies information about the mark, such as the serial number and the mark itself; the person or entity assigning the trademark and the person or entity receiving the trademark; and the rights that are being assigned. Typically, the party receiving the assignment will record the assignment with the USPTO. All of the documents submitted for recordation must meet the following requirements:

- They must be legible.
- They must be in English or be accompanied by a translation into English.
- Only one side of each page should be used.
- The paper used should be flexible, strong, white, nonshiny, and durable.
- The paper should preferably be no larger than 21.6 x 33.1 cm (8 x 14 inches) with a 2.5 cm (one-inch) margin on all sides.

When submitting an assignment for recordation, the appropriate fee must also be paid. This fee can vary

but at the time of writing this book, the fee is $40 per recordation.

Each document that is filed with the USPTO for recordation must include a cover sheet. You can download the cover sheet from the USPTO website at www.uspto.gov/web/forms/.

The Least You Need to Know

- Ownership in a trademark is established by use.
- Ownership in a trademark can be expanded nationwide by registering the trademark with the federal government.
- Failure to register a trademark with the federal government can allow others to use and gain rights in and to your trademark.
- When a trademark is assigned to you, you should immediately record the assignment with the U.S. Patent and Trademark Office.
- You cannot assign or sell a trademark that is the subject of an intent-to-use application.

International Trademarks

In This Chapter

- An overview of international trademark protection
- The ins and outs of the Madrid Protocol
- Advantages and disadvantages of the Madrid Protocol
- Other options in international filing

Habla español? Sprechen Sie deutsch? Parlez vous français?

Trademarks that are used and registered in the United States do not create any rights in any foreign countries. Likewise, trademarks that are registered in other countries are not granted any rights in the United States. However, as our markets and trade grow, our world shrinks. Thus, companies that traditionally were only based in the United States are branching out with an international presence. How do you obtain registration of your trademark in foreign countries?

You have learned that it is very easy to expand your trademark rights in the United States simply by registering the trademark with the U.S. Patent and Trademark Office (USPTO). However, if you plan on going international with your business, what are your options for protecting your valuable trademarks in other countries and for expanding your ownership in the trademarks to include other countries?

Suppose you have registered a trademark in the United States. Is it possible for someone else to register that same mark in another country? Yes it is. The geocentric characteristic of trademark protection makes this a very valid concern. International treaties, such as the Madrid Protocol, help to alleviate the problems that can arise with concurrent trademark registration in a global economy.

In this chapter, we describe how to register your trademarks in other countries and what options you have for registering your trademarks.

Overview of International Trademarks

A trademark that is registered in the United States only provides you protection against others using your trademark within the United States. To gain trademark rights in another country, it is necessary to secure trademark rights in that country, under the laws of that country. There is much similarity

in the trademark laws of various countries; however, there are also some substantial differences.

One of the biggest differences between trademark law in the United States and other countries is that in the United States, trademark rights come into existence upon the first use of the trademark in commerce. This is very different than most of the world. Outside of the United States, trademark rights are usually obtained as a result of registering the trademark—not using the trademark.

When examining international trademark law, it is necessary to observe three perspectives. The first perspective is when you have a registered U.S. mark that you want to protect in other countries. The second perspective is when you have a registered trademark in another country that you want to protect in the United States. The third perspective is when you do not have a registered trademark, but you want to file for registration in several countries.

Going International with Your Trademark

If you have filed an application for trademark registration in the United States, you can file an international application based on the U.S. trademark application. If you file the international application within six months of filing the U.S. application, you can claim priority to the U.S. application under the Paris Convention. Claiming priority to the U.S. application means that the application filed in

another country will be treated as though it was filed at the same time the U.S. application was filed. This is important due to the fact that most foreign countries do not have a use requirement for registering trademarks. Thus, if you publicly use a trademark in the United States, someone can register that mark in another country even if they are not using the mark. Once you file a U.S. application, that date can be used against subsequent applicants in other countries.

Just the Facts _____

Because the deadline to file a foreign application based on the filing date of your U.S. application is six months, you might have to file your foreign applications before you know if the trademark can be registered in the United States.

Foreign Marks Coming to the United States

An application for trademark registration that has been filed in another country may serve as the basis for a U.S. trademark application. If the U.S. application is filed within six months of filing the foreign application, the U.S. application can claim priority to the foreign application under the Paris Convention. This six-month window of time should be considered when conducting a trademark search prior to filing a U.S. application. You should examine at least the last six months of foreign filings.

Filing of an International Trademark Application

You can file for a trademark application in each individual country in which you seek protection, or you can file a single application under one or more of the group filing agreements. There are advantages and disadvantages for each of these two options, and you do not have to exclusively rely on just one option.

Individual Country Filing

Similar to filing an application for trademark registration in the United States, you can also file for registration in other individual countries. Registering your trademark in other countries secures your protection and ownership of the trademark within that county; however, if you plan on doing business in a large number of countries, the cost of registering your trademark in each country can be quite expensive.

When filing for protection in individual countries, you must identify a foreign associate from each country in which you desire to file. If you are working through an attorney, your attorney should have a list of foreign associates that he or she has previously used for such services. The foreign associate is necessary because typically, your U.S. attorney will not be licensed to practice law in the foreign jurisdiction.

The foreign associate, similar to your U.S. attorney, will interface with the appropriate government authorities in the particular country in an effort to obtain registration of your trademark.

So what kind of costs are we talking about for international trademark protection? The costs can vary from country to country depending on the government filing fees, the attorney fees of the foreign associate, and the work involved by your U.S. attorney in coordinating the efforts working with the foreign associates. However, in general you should expect to spend around $2,000 for each registration. If you want worldwide protection, then you are looking at filing in around 200 countries. Doing the math you would be looking at around $400,000 to apply for worldwide protection.

One-Stop Shopping—Group Filing

Another option for international filing is to do a group filing. A group filing allows you to file a single application for the registration of a trademark that can be applied to multiple countries. The group filing options generally are created through agreements that are entered into by various countries. The agreements set forth rules and regulations that the member countries must adhere to, and as a result, uniform treatment of trademark rights can be obtained throughout the member countries.

Currently, there is no single agreement or group that includes all of the countries throughout the

world. However, if you desire to file only in a select few countries and those countries are included in one or more of the international filing groups then you are in luck.

A few of the international filing groups and the countries belonging to those groups are provided below. However, please understand that the member countries can change from time to time and you should seek advice of counsel to determine the current member countries.

Madrid Protocol

Albania	Finland
Antigua and Barbuda	France
Armenia	Georgia
Australia	Germany
Austria	Greece
Belarus	Hungary
Benelux (Belgium, Netherlands and Luxembourg)	Iceland
	Iran, Islamic Republic of
Bhutan	Ireland
Bulgaria	Italy
China	Japan
Cuba	Kenya
Cyprus	Korea, The Democratic People's Republic of
Czech Republic	
Denmark	Korea, The Republic of
Estonia	Latvia

Lesotho

Liechtenstein

Lithuania

Macedonia, The former Republic of Yugoslav

Moldova, Republic of Monaco

Mongolia

Morocco

Mozambique

Netherlands Antilles

Norway

Poland

Portugal

Romania

Russian Federation

Serbia and Montenegro

Sierra Leone

Singapore

Slovakia

Slovenia

Spain

Swaziland

Sweden

Switzerland

Turkey

Turkmenistan

United Kingdom

United States of America

Ukraine

Zambia

European Union's Community Trade Mark (CTM)

Austria

Belgium

Denmark

Finland

France

Germany

Greece

Ireland

Italy

Luxembourg

Netherlands

Portugal

Spain

Sweden

The United Kingdom

African Regional Industrial Property Association (ARIPO)

Botswana

Gambia

Ghana

Kenya

Lesotho

Malawi

Mozambique

Sierra Leone

Somalia

Sudan

Swaziland

Tanzania, United Republic of

Uganda

Zambia and Zimbabwe

The African Intellectual Property Organization (AIPO)

Benin

Burkina Faso

Cameroon

Central African Republic

Chad

Congo (Brazzaville)

Equatorial Guinea

Guinea-Bissau

Gabon

Guinea

Ivory Coast

Mali

Mauritania

Niger

Senegal

Togo

The World Intellectual Property Organization (WIPO)

The World Intellectual Property Organization (WIPO) is an administrative arm of the United

Nations. WIPO was developed to support international trade and to promote reciprocity of IP recognition and protection among various nations. The WIPO administers the Madrid Protocol and the Paris Convention.

Information about the WIPO can be obtained from the organization's website at www.wipo.int.

The Paris Convention

The Paris Convention for the Protection of Industrial Property was signed into effect in 1883 and a revised version was introduced on July 14, 1967. A primary purpose of the Paris Convention is that it obligates member nations to provide substantive protection for the procurement, maintenance, and enforcement of industrial property. Specifically, the Paris Convention requires member nations to, among other things:

- Implement a trademark registration system that offers protection against infringement and unfair competition
- Recognize the filing date of a trademark application filed in a home member nation as the priority date in another member nation as long as the application is filed within six months of the home nation application
- Confer equal rights to all trademark owners, whether foreign or domestic

The Madrid Protocol

The Madrid Protocol is a part of the Madrid Agreement Concerning the International Registration of Marks. The Madrid Protocol is an international treaty that allows a trademark owner to seek registration in any of the countries that have joined the Madrid Protocol. The trademark owner can file a single application, called an "international application."

The United States became a member of the Madrid Protocol on November 2, 2003. The Madrid Protocol is part of several agreements that, in general, is directed toward the international registration of trademarks. Under the Madrid Protocol, you can file a single application for registering a trademark in one country but have the protection apply within each country that is a member of the Madrid Protocol. There are advantages and disadvantages associated with filing an application for trademark registration under the Madrid Protocol.

Filing an International Trademark Under the Madrid Protocol

An International Trademark application filed under the Madrid Protocol is based on a trademark application filed in one of the countries that is a member of the Madrid Protocol. Thus, for U.S. companies or citizens, you can file an international trademark application based on an application that has been filed with the USPTO. The U.S. trademark

application is referred to as the "basic application" and any U.S. registration that is obtained for a basic application is referred to as a "basic registration." If you are not a U.S. citizen or national, you can also file a trademark application in another country and have that application serve as your basic application.

When filing an international trademark application, the trademark and the owner of the application must be the same as in the basic application or registration. The international application may be based on more than one USPTO application or registration, provided the mark and the owner are the same for each basic application or registration. In addition, the goods or services identified in the international trademark application must be the same, or a subset of, the goods or services listed in the basic application.

U.S. companies and individuals must file the international trademark application with the USPTO.

Filing Requirements

To meet the minimum requirements, the international trademark application must include or identify:

- The filing date and serial number of the basic application or the registration date and registration number of the basic registration

- The name of the international applicant; this name must be the same as the applicant or registrant in the basic application or basic registration

- The current address of the applicant
- A reproduction of the mark (in color if appropriate)
- A description of the mark
- An indication of the type of mark
- A list of the goods or services; this must be identical to or narrower than the list of goods or services in each claimed basic application or registration
- A list of the countries selected (the countries must be a member of the Madrid Protocol, referred to as a contracting party)
- The certification fee, the international application fees for all classes, and the fees for all designated contracting parties
- A statement that the applicant is entitled to file an international application in the office, specifying that the applicant: is a national of the United States; has a domicile in the United States; or has a real and effective industrial or commercial establishment in the United States
- An e-mail address for receipt of correspondence from the office

The international applicant must pay the U.S. certification fee(s) at the time of submission and identify at least one Contracting Party in which an extension of protection (that is, registration in a Contracting Party) is sought.

Cost for Filing Under the Madrid Protocol

The cost for filing an international application includes:

- Certification fee of $100 per class if the international application is based on a single basic application/registration
- Certification fee of $150 per class if the international application is based on multiple basic applications/registrations
- Basic filing fee of around $530 ($734 if the mark claims particular colors)
- Supplementary fee of $60 for each classification of goods and/or services beyond three
- Complimentary fee of around $60 for each contracting country selected

The actual fees are paid in Swiss francs, and thus these actual U.S. dollar figures are only approximate.

Processing of International Application

The USPTO verifies the completeness of the application and then forwards the application to the International Bureau. If the international application does not meet the minimum requirements, then the USPTO will not certify the international application. The USPTO will then notify the international applicant of the reasons why the international application cannot be certified. The certification fee is not refundable. The international applicant may promptly resubmit a corrected

international application based on the same U.S. application or registration. The certification fees must be included with the new submission.

Once an international application is submitted to the International Bureau, the International Bureau reviews the application to determine whether it meets the Madrid Protocol filing requirements. If the requirements are met and the fees paid, the International Bureau will then register the mark, publish it in the *WIPO Gazette of International Marks (WIPO Gazette)*, send a certificate to the international applicant, and notify the Offices of the contracting parties designated in the international application.

If the Madrid Protocol filing requirements have not been met, the International Bureau will send a notice to both the USPTO and the international applicant that explains the problems with the application. If the problems are corrected within the prescribed time, the International Bureau will register the mark.

Under the Paris Convention, the priority date of the international application can be based on the U.S. application, even if the filing of the U.S. application was before the United States became a member of the Madrid Protocol. To obtain the priority date, the international application must:

- Assert a claim of priority.
- Be filed in the USPTO within six months after the filing date of the basic application.

When the International Bureau registers the mark, the International Bureau will notify each country identified in the international registration of the request for an extension of protection to that country. Each identified country will then examine the request for an extension of protection the same as it would a national application under its laws. If the application meets the requirements for registration of that country, then the country will grant protection of the mark in its country.

Advantages of the Madrid Protocol

There are several advantages for filing of an international trademark application under the Madrid Protocol. These advantages include:

- A single application can be filed to register the mark in many countries.
- The fees for filing are much less than filing in each country individually.
- A common set of filing requirements are applied.
- Each country must examine the application within 18 months of the international filing date.
- Renewals are accomplished by filing a single document and fee.
- Changing applicant information or assignment recordations can be accomplished in a single filing.

Disadvantages of the Madrid Protocol

There are several disadvantages for filing of an international trademark application under the Madrid Protocol. These disadvantages include:

- The international application is dependent on the U.S. basic application during the first five years of registration. Thus, if the basic application is refused, withdrawn, cancelled, or restricted, in whole or in part, then the International Bureau will cancel the international registration.

- Use of the mark is required when filing the U.S. basic application; however, if you file directly in individual countries, this use is not required.

- The goods and services descriptions must be the same or narrower, thus the more strict requirements imposed on the descriptions of goods and services required in U.S. trademark registrations will limit the breadth of the international registrations based on the U.S. basic application.

- The Madrid Protocol currently does not include many Western Hemisphere countries, such as Canada, Mexico, and South American countries.

The European Union's Community Trade Mark (CTM)

The European Union's Community Trade Mark (CTM) system went into effect in 1996 and included 15 nations. It is expected to grow to include the entire European Community. Although you might still obtain registrations in each country of the European Community, the CTM allows you to file a single community-wide trademark application. The applicant can save considerable costs in filing a CTM application. The CTM is relatively new, and thus it has not been proven by the test of time. One disadvantage of the CTM is that entire CTM application can be defeated by prior national rights in just one member nation. Thus, it is very important to search for prior rights before deciding to proceed with an application.

The African Regional Industrial Property Association (ARIPO)

The African Regional Industrial Property Organization (ARIPO) is an international organization created in December 1976. The purpose of the ARIPO is to enable African countries to pool their resources in order to avoid duplication of financial and human resources. The ARIPO adheres to the Banjul Protocol that establishes a centralized filing system where a single application in one language can be filed with the ARIPO to obtain protection of a trademark in several countries in southern Africa. After the

application is verified for correctness, it is forwarded to the member countries, each of which will have 12 months to examine the application. If no objections are raised by the various countries, the ARIPO will register the mark as in effect for all designated countries.

The ARIPO does not supplant the ability to file an application directly into one of its member countries, and the ARIPO system does not handle post application procedures such as oppositions, cancellations, and infringements.

The African Intellectual Property Organisation (AIPO)

The African Intellectual Property Organisation (AIPO) enables a centralized filing for trademark protection various former French colonies of Africa. Aside from the AIPO, it is not possible to obtain national registrations in these countries. Within the AIPO, only the first applicant is entitled to registration. A prior user may object to a registration within six months after the filing of the application if the applicant was acting in bad faith.

An AIPO application may claim priority under the Paris Convention and it conforms to the international classification system.

Upon receiving an application, the AIPO examines the application as to form and inherent registrability. The AIPO does not check against former registrations. Thus, an owner of a mark in an AIPO country

should monitor the registry to determine if someone files an application for a similar mark, and if so, must file an opposition within six months of the publication of the trademark.

> **Just the Facts**
>
> The Nairobi Treaty, which was adopted on September 26, 1981, provides special protection to the Olympic Symbol.

The Least You Need to Know

- Filing an application for trademark registration in the United States does not give you any rights in other countries.

- You can obtain the priority date of a U.S. trademark application for foreign trademark applications if you file the foreign application within six months of filing the U.S. application.

- Under the Madrid Protocol, you can file a single application with the USPTO and have the trademark registered in any of the member countries.

- You can elect to individually file a trademark application in almost any country.

Making Money off of Trademarks

In This Chapter

- Licensing your valuable marks to others
- Finding the right mark to license for your product or service
- How to come up with the right price for a license or sale of a mark

We've covered all of what you need to know to protect your trademark, as well as the benefits effective protection can have on your marketing of goods and services. However, what you may not realize is that a successful brand or mark can be used to promote goods and services affiliated with other companies.

Trademark licensing is a growing marketplace, reaping great rewards for both sides of the transaction. However, in these situations, you must take steps to ensure you're not being unduly

disadvantaged. These pitfalls may include simply missing out on a few bucks, providing an exclusive license to a company that never earns you a dime, and even, potentially, losing rights to your trademark.

In this chapter, we're going to help you understand the basics of trademark licensing from both sides of the negotiating table, and provide you with some jewels of information that will make the other side sit up and take notice.

Licensing of Trademarks

The expression *intellectual property* contains the word *property*. As a result, you can treat intellectual property just like any other property. You can rent it (called a *license*) or, as you learned earlier, sell it (called an *assignment*). If you're going to license your trademark, you need to decide under what terms you will license it. Or you may be considering licensing a mark from another company, which raises other issues. We'll cover both situations next.

Licensing Your Mark

For purposes of this section, let's consider this example. You are a construction firm and came up with a great idea for a line of clothing called *JackHammer*. You read this book and took the steps to obtain a trademark registration for *JackHammer* in connection with a wide variety of clothes items (for example, hats, pants, and shirts). You've

produced and sold these clothes to your customers
for a period of time and suddenly another company
comes up to you and says that they want to license
the *JackHammer* name for a line of clothing they
intend to create. It sounds interesting, but you're
wondering what things you should cover in the
trademark license agreement.

- **License.** You are entering into a licensing
  relationship between you (the *licensor*) and
  the company (the *licensee*). The licensee will
  have the right to use *JackHammer* in connection with the sale of clothing. You may even
  want to further limit the license to a specific
  type of clothing (for example, shirts) so that
  you can license *JackHammer* for other types
  of clothing like pants and jackets. Therefore,
  the license that you provide to the licensee
  has to be focused (and limited) on what the
  licensee will be doing with the mark.

 Legal-Ease _____

Licensee refers to the individual who is
licensing a mark *from* another person.
Licensor is the term for the person who is
licensing a mark *to* another person.

- **Tying the license to the goods or services
  covered.** Remember that federally registered marks are tied to the goods or services
  described in the registration. As a result, you
  should not permit the licensee to use your

mark in connection with inappropriate goods or services. For example, you would not be able to license the mark *JackHammer* in connection with the introduction of a new car. Your mark is, in no way, connected to the sale of automobiles. To combat this and potentially offer licenses of your mark for other types of products in the future, you should file intent-to-use applications related to other goods and services. Please keep in mind, though, that you will not be able to file an allegation of use until your licensee releases its goods or services with your mark attached. Please note, however, that you still cannot assign an intent-to-use mark, unless it's in connection with the sale of your business.

- **Money.** You can request some payment up front for the right to license your mark or you may just want to make money each time the product is sold with your mark attached to it. Perhaps you can negotiate for both. Typically, this is a risk/reward analysis. You could probably make more money from sale royalties, assuming that the licensor is successful in marketing the clothing. However, if you prefer safe money—otherwise known as *up-front money*—you'll probably settle for less (but at least you know you'll get something!). You should also request the right to audit the books and records of the licensee to ensure that they're reporting the licensing revenue to you accurately.

- **Exclusivity.** Will anyone else be permitted to license the mark? You need to decide whether the license will be exclusive or not to the licensee. If you do decide to make the license exclusive, you should consider whether the exclusivity is tied to any performance requirements (such as the sale of goods).

- **Business model.** What happens if the licensee sells the trademarked product as part of an overall kit or system? What percentage of the purchase price should be allocated to the trademarked product that you receive royalties on? For example, let's assume I license *JackHammer* to go onto shirts and I receive 5 percent of all sales on those shirts, but the licensee sells the shirts as part of an entire outfit, such as with pants, shoes, and a hat. Let's also assume that I don't receive a royalty on any of these other clothes items because they don't have the *JackHammer* brand on them. How do I know what amount of the sales price should be attributed to the shirts? In fact, the licensee may claim that only a dollar is related to the shirt and the other $99 is for the other components. Bottom line, make sure you get agreement up front.

- **Quality and consistency.** One of the most important terms you must have in your license agreement is minimum requirements for quality and consistent use of your mark.

In the absence of your insistence on a consistent quality of goods or services associated with your mark, consumers will get differing products and services. If consumers get a different quality of goods and services, then your mark is failing to achieve its most important objective—to help consumers identify the source of origin of the goods or services. This failure may lead to an abandonment of your rights in the mark. As part of the quality and consistency requirement, you should make sure you have a right to inspect how the brand is being utilized, including visiting their factories and resellers and reviewing their advertising, brochures, signs, and other materials that contain the licensed mark. Make sure you have the ability to influence the use or terminate the agreement if you're not satisfied with it.

- **Customer complaints.** The licensee should be required to provide you with notice of any customer complaints relating to trademarked products. You'll want to know this information to ensure appropriate quality is being associated with your trademark.

- **Continued ownership.** Although you may have exclusively licensed the mark, you still own it! Therefore, you need to state this in the agreement so it's completely clear.

- **Notification of infringement.** Because the company that licenses your mark will be out in the marketplace, they may be in the best

position to observe other companies infringing your mark. If they come across any infringers, they should notify you immediately and let you know as much as possible about the perpetrators so you can take action against them.

- **Term.** For how long are you going to let the company use your mark? If the person is unsuccessful, you should have the ability to end the relationship and either do it yourself or engage with someone who can sell the product more successfully. As the trademark owner, you have a tremendous amount of flexibility due to your ability to terminate a license agreement. Many individuals have entered into a licensing arrangement only to realize later that they received less than they could have.

- **Geography.** Where can the seller distribute the products with your trademark? In your town, across the state, or across the country? Or internationally? You may want to consider limiting the seller to a specific territory so that you can engage with additional potential licensees in other areas.

When You're the One Taking a License

Why would you ever want to license another company's trademark? It's often difficult to break into a marketplace with a product or service. You have to educate your customers not only about the product

or service, but also your company. The license of a popular brand may help you avoid many of these hurdles and put you on the fast track to success. A great example of this might be the license of a popular local telephone service to an upstart alarm company. If consumers in an area trust the phone service, they'll feel a level of comfort with an alarm service under the same name.

Now that you understand why, let's tackle how! We've already covered a variety of factors in a license agreement important to the licensor. You should review these factors because they're equally important to you and you should be prepared for the licensor's insistence on these points.

Make Sure You Get It All

You may recall the related concepts of trademarks and trade dress. A trademark may be only one piece of what you're interested in licensing. For example, you may want to open a pirate-themed restaurant with the trademarked name *StowAway*. If you license the name, you may not get all of the rights you intended. You may also want to license the entire trade dress, which might include the color scheme of the restaurant, the look of the servers' uniforms, and the decorations around the restaurant.

Watch Out, It Can Be Tricky!

As we explained, this is just a quick list of items to consider when licensing to or from someone. We do recommend consulting an attorney before you enter

into a licensing arrangement. In Chapter 12, we go through some of the things you should consider when hiring an attorney, so check it out.

So, What Is a Trademark Worth?

You're probably wondering how to value a trademark or brand. Up front, you should realize it's not a perfect science as a trademark, by definition, is unique to the goods and services of a particular company. This is in contrast to a product that can be mass produced. Many individuals can bid on the mass-produced product to arrive at a fair value for it.

When you're trying to value a trademark for purposes of selling that mark, there are a few methods used by valuation experts. However, if you're licensing the mark, it's another story. Just because you arrive at the overall value of a brand or trademark does not make it obvious what you should charge for a license. However, armed with the valuation information, you can at least decide whether the price is in the ballpark. Also, valuation information is useful for deciding whether to charge some up-front amount (which may be a good idea if the deal is speculative) or focus entirely on a contingency based on a licensee's sales. Of course, you must remember that a contingency might amount to no revenue and you should have the ability to terminate the agreement or, at least, make it non-exclusive in such an event. In any event, let's go through the various valuation methods.

Valuation Methods

There are three basic approaches: cost to replace, market, and income. The *cost to replace* approach is the amount it would take to create a comparable mark that's as highly regarded and useful. Therefore, to figure this out, you would need to take into account all of the marketing and development costs spent to create the brand (assuming all the same costs would need to be undertaken today).

The *market* approach tries to determine how much it would cost to license the mark if someone else owned it. Of course, this method is hard under the current circumstances, because that's precisely what we're trying to figure out! However, if you're Coke and you want to figure out how much to charge a collectibles company that wants to license your brand, you could try to calculate the amount that Pepsi would charge you for a license to their brand for collectibles. The general concept behind this approach is that value has been created from owning the trademark, and now you don't have to go out in the market and license it.

The *income* approach is today's value of all the money you're making from a particular mark. This is sometimes difficult to figure out, but can be a pretty powerful indication of value when done correctly. In the following section, we discuss the Interbrand® approach, which is a modified version of the income approach and a very popular one in the marketplace.

The Interbrand® Approach

Interbrand® is a company that assesses values of brands for a variety of companies. Interbrand® approaches valuation by first calculating the total annual sales of the company (or segment specifically associated with the brand). For example, GE has numerous divisions, including NBC. Therefore, if you're assessing the value of the NBC brand, you would only look to sales in that division. From that number, you subtract an amount related to the tangible assets in a company (these could include equipment, inventory, and like items). The resulting number Interbrand® equates to the *intangibles* value. From this amount, Interbrand® conducts a variety of research and interviews to determine what amount of the remaining amount should be equated with the brand value.

Legal-Ease

Intangibles are items that are not physical in form. A brand is not something you can pick up and hold—it is something that consumers connect with your product or service.

Pure Profit Licensing

Many companies are beginning to realize the vast opportunity that they have in licensing brands. Because a tremendous investment has already been

made in making a brand either generally famous (such as Coke) or well-known in a very specific niche (such as cigars), the opportunities to make money off of the brand become clear. For example, for years Coke has licensed its brand to a number of companies to create collectibles, clothing, and a variety of other products. A cigar maker might be able to license its brand for a new lighter company, beer company, or poker chip company. Trademark licensing is a rapidly growing part of many companies' business models. Most important, brand licensing can be very profitable as there is little if any additional cost associated with entering into a license (as we said, the investment has already been made).

The Least You Need to Know

- Just like with regular property, you can license or sell intellectual property.
- There are many elements to a trademark license agreement that require consideration.
- Brand licensing can be a very profitable opportunity for a company.

The Web and Lawyers

In This Chapter

- Online resources for trademarks
- Domain name resources
- Swimming with the sharks (lawyers)

We've covered a ton about trademarks in this book. However, there are a few more items that are worth mentioning before you're a self-proclaimed trademark expert.

First, we want to direct you to some important online resources that can provide you with further information and assistance in your trademark and domain name endeavors. In this chapter, we briefly describe a few key websites. Of course, there are others sprouting up every day and we always appreciate hearing about them, so please e-mail us if you come across any. (Our contact e-mail is included with our bios on the inside back cover of this book.)

Finally, there are always situations where it makes sense to enlist a lawyer. In this chapter, we give you helpful hints in choosing the right lawyer for your

trademark needs and, potentially, other intellectual property needs.

Online Trademark Resources

There are many websites that provide you with excellent additional information regarding trademarks—in the United States and abroad. Of course, you can always mail or e-mail us—the authors—should you have any questions and we'll be pleased to point you in the right direction. Also, we provide a variety of resources, including a periodic electronic newsletter that you can sign up for through our website at www.lavagroup.net.

Government Agencies

Government agencies, both domestic and foreign, can provide significant benefits to users. For example, the U.S. Patent and Trademark Office (USPTO) website permits you to file a wide variety of documents electronically. This saves considerable time and expense and is the preferred mode of communications by the USPTO. We wanted to provide you with several sites that are worth your time. You'll be able to dive deeper on most of the topics covered in this book.

The Mother of Trademark Websites

The official U.S. governmental website for trademarks (the USPTO) is www.uspto.gov. From this site, you can access a vast array of resources. When

you arrive at www. uspto.gov, select **Trademarks** and you will be taken to a new page that breaks down trademark information into a variety of categories:

- Basics
- Madrid Protocol
- Manuals and Publications
- Laws and Regulations
- Get a Trademark Registration
- Keep a Trademark Registration
- Trademark Trial and Appeal Board
- Resources
- eBusiness

Almost everything you need to know can be found on this site. The USPTO publishes a variety of resources and circulars itself that can be accessed through the site. These items often contain analysis and descriptions of changes to the trademark law as well as interpretations of specific regulations. Because these resources are published by the USPTO, they have a high degree of reliability (as opposed to some outside person's interpretation of the law).

Another important feature is the search component (accessed under a few tabs, including Get a Trademark Registration). From this link, you'll be able to search records of trademark registrations. The search criteria can be broken down into a variety of categories, including the words, filing date, owner, serial number, whether the mark is live or dead, and many more criteria.

Just the Facts

The USPTO now *encourages* applicants to do as much electronically as possible. Terrorist acts such as the anthrax scare have increased fear of receipt of regular mail. The trademark examiners also attempt to communicate with applicants and their attorneys via e-mail whenever possible.

World Intellectual Property Organization

The World Intellectual Property Organization (www.wipo.org) is one of the specialized units of the United Nations and focuses on enforcing 23 international treaties related to intellectual property (including the Madrid Protocol and the Trademark Law Treaty).

Office for Harmonization in the Internal Market

The Office of Harmonization in the Internal Market (OHIM) can be found at oami.eu.int/en/default.htm. OHIM registers *community trademarks* and *community designs* which are then valid throughout the European Community. Registration provides registrants with exclusive rights so that they may prohibit others from using their marks and designs in commercial or industrial activities in this region.

U.S. and International Associations

There are associations in the United States and abroad that provide excellent reference information so that you can learn more about intellectual property and obtain helpful resources. We have indicated a couple of them below.

The American Intellectual Property Law Association (AIPLA)

The American Intellectual Property Law Association (AIPLA) can be found at www.aipla.org. The AIPLA is more than 100 years old and focuses on ensuring that IP lawyers maintain high ethical standards, improve legislation relating to intellectual property matters, and educate the public on these matters.

International Trademark Association (INTA)

The International Trademark Association (INTA) can be found at www.inta.org. INTA is a nonprofit organization with more than 4,000 members from over 170 different countries. INTA's mission is focused on "the support and advancement of trademarks and related intellectual property as elements of fair and effective national and international commerce." The organization formed more than 125 years ago to shape and advance appropriate legislation and education. If you're interested in joining, please read through their website. There are many opportunities to get involved in numerous

committees that are generally focused on one of three areas: INTA corporate and membership matters, education, and policy advancement.

Trademark Search Services

As we've described, it is often useful to conduct a trademark search (called a *clearance search*) before you invest a significant amount of money into a brand or registering a trademark. There are several firms that can conduct these searches, including LawMart (www.lawmart.com), AllMark Trademark (www.allmarktrademark.com), and Visomark (www.visomark.com). However, one of the oldest, largest, and most well-known authorities on conducting comprehensive searches is the firm of Thomson & Thomson (www.thomson-thomson.com). These firms can conduct domestic or national searches and can also provide clearance searches for domain names. It typically takes a week to receive your results and a clearance search will cost from $400 to $600, an amount that might seem significant now but is really very low if you were forced to change your name or mark because it infringes on an existing mark.

Good Counsel

Even marks that have not been federally registered can cause problems. Therefore, it's always a good idea to search for similar marks in public use before you fall in love with a particular name.

Obtaining a Domain Name

There are a variety of sites from which you can register a domain name. Remember, it pays to see whether a domain name is available before you register your trademark (if you want your trademark and domain name to be the same). The reverse is also true. It sometimes doesn't make sense to register a trademark if the domain name is not available.

Internet Corporation for Assigned Names and Numbers

As we mentioned in Chapter 8, the Internet Corporation for Assigned Names and Numbers (ICANN) is the governing organization charged with providing other companies with the right to issue domain names and related issues. Some of the sites you can use to check on domain name availability (and subsequent registration) are:

- Register.com at www.register.com
- Verisign at www.verisign.com
- GoDaddy at www.godaddy.com
- Verio at www.verio.com
- Domain Direct at www.domaindirect.com

Using an Attorney

We mentioned earlier in this book that it might not be necessary to use an attorney for registering a trademark with the USPTO. There can be benefits,

however, to using an attorney for registration. An attorney's experience drafting an appropriate description of goods and services as well as negotiating with a trademark examiner can be very helpful and ensure you obtain the broadest possible protection for your mark. Also, when it comes to matters such as an opposition, trademark infringement, or licensing of a trademark, using an attorney is likely necessary. Therefore, we want to take you through some of the benefits of using an attorney in your trademark registration matters:

- **Greater assurances.** While the information in this book should get you through the trademark registration process as well as introduce you to a variety of other important issues and considerations, it's always good to have someone who is an expert on trademark issues. If you do not hire an attorney to take care of a trademark registration, you may be able to request a quick review to make sure you did everything properly. This should not cost too much and may give you the added assurance you need.

- **"Safehouse" for your registration records.** For trademark registrations, your attorney likely maintains organized files including the correspondence sent to and received from the USPTO, which can be helpful if there's ever a dispute as to who developed the trademarked work.

- **Docketing of your trademark application and registration.** As you've learned, there

are many critical dates that arise after filing of a trademark application, such as the dates for filing a foreign registration, an allegation of use, and renewals.

- **Involvement in related matters.** Often times, the process of registering a trademark or dealing with another trademark issue is only one part of a much larger effort you're undertaking (for example, registering a mark may also be related to forming a company, entering into a contract for services, and so on). If this is the case, it is probably a good idea to have an attorney assist you in the overall process to ensure that you fully understand your rights and obligations.

Picking an Attorney

Choosing the right attorney for your trademark matter really depends on a variety of matters and what you believe you'll need from the attorney in the long run.

References

In every service profession there are good, okay, and downright bad professionals. With respect to intellectual property professionals, this rule holds true. Therefore, it is important that you do your homework and select an attorney who has *demonstrated* the ability to handle the work you will ask him or her to do. The best way to do this is to obtain a referral from someone you trust who has worked

with the attorney in the past on a related matter. In the absence of a personal referral, you should ask the attorney for two or three references.

In addition to references, you should ask the attorney questions related to each of the other topics in this section (time, cost, docketing, experience in a related matter, and personality).

Time

One of the biggest complaints about attorneys is their responsiveness to a client's needs. Failure to handle a client's request in a timely manner is usually because of the lawyer's busy schedule. Therefore, you should reach agreement on the exact information that the lawyer needs from you and the time frame for filing a trademark registration once the information is submitted. Then, hold him or her to it. The same applies for any other tasks that you may request of the lawyer.

Experience in Related Matters

As we stated earlier, a trademark issue may be part of a larger effort you are undertaking, such as launching a business. You may also have other forms of intellectual property you want to protect (such as patents or copyrights). If this is the case, you may need more specialized knowledge in the area of intellectual property. There are many attorneys who, either individually or through their law firm, can provide a full array of intellectual property services. If you believe a trademark is the only

type of intellectual property protection you will seek and you are forming a new business or have other on-going legal needs related to your business, you should make sure that the lawyer, or the firm at which he or she practices, handles this type of corporate transactional work. To ensure that the attorney handling your trademark registration is qualified, you should ask the attorney specific questions regarding his or her experiences, with specific emphasis on trademark issues including whether the firm is able to docket the trademark application and ensure that critical dates are not missed.

Personality Fit

One item that is often overlooked is the personality fit between the client and the attorney. Many people possess preconceived notions about the personalities of attorneys. They're tough, overopinionated, nerdy, sarcastic, introverted, extroverted, or worse! In reality, there are different personalities of lawyers and you can find one that fits your unique needs. Most important, you should feel comfortable to approach and discuss any matter with your attorney and know that he or she will respond to you in a quick and informative way.

Cost

The most important item to a client is typically the cost of an attorney. It is also likely the reason that many individuals want to file their own trademark applications. Please make sure you consider the

other factors and benefits described above. Trademark efforts are typically broken down into a variety of actions, such as conducting a trademark search, reviewing the search results, preparing and filing an application, and responding to communications from the Trademark Office to ensure that registration is obtained. That being said, you should request a flat fee quote for the application process (through filing) and the following up communications and compare that to other providers. Our research shows that attorneys charge from $500 to $1,500 to file an application and $500 to $1,000 for minor follow-up. If issues arise during the registration process, costs can rise substantially.

The Least You Need to Know

- There are many great online resources to increase your knowledge about trademarks and keep you up to date on any changes.

- Domain names should be checked before you file your trademark registration, to make sure you can get the domain of your choice.

- It is often helpful to use an attorney on your trademark matters.

Appendix A

Further Reading

Elias, Stephen. *Trademark: Legal Care for Your Business Product Name*. Berkley, CA: Nolo Press, 2003.

Elias, Stephen, and Patricia Gima. *Domain Names: How to Choose and Protect a Great Name for Your Website*. Berkley, CA: Nolo Press, 2000.

Elias, Stephen, and Richard Stim. *Patent, Copyright and Trademark: An Intellectual Property Desk Reference*. Berkley, CA: Nolo Press, 2003.

Isenberg, Doug. *GigaLaw Guide to Internet Law*. New York: Random House Trade Paperbacks, 2002.

Kera, David J., and Theodore H. Davis Jr. *2003 Trademark Law Handbook*. New York: International Trademark Association, 2003.

Rony, Ellen, and Peter Roney. *The Domain Name Handbook: High Stakes and Strategies in Cyberspace*. Lawrence, KS: R&D Books, 1998.

Warda, Mark, James Rogers, and Ron Idra. *How to Register Your Trademark, 3rd Edition*. Naperville, IL: Sourcebooks Trade, 2000.

Wilson, Lee. *The Trademark Guide*. New York: Allworth Press, 1998.

Glossary

abandoned   Occurs when a trademark becomes generic or its use is discontinued.

affidavit   Refers to a written declaration or statement that is made under oath and before a notary public or authorized officer.

affixation   Refers to connecting a mark's use with either the goods (the mark must appear on the goods, the container for the goods, or displays associated with the goods) or the services (the mark must be used or displayed in the sale or advertising of the services).

African Intellectual Property Organisation (AIPO)   An organization for centralized filing for trademark protection in various former French colonies of Africa.

African Regional Industrial Property Organization (ARIPO)   An international organization created for the purpose of the enabling a single trademark application to be filed for several African countries.

Anticybersquatting Consumer Protection Act (ACPA) An act authorizing trademark owners to sue cybersquatters and force them to transfer the domain name back to the owner.

appeal A process to challenge an examining attorney's refusal to register your trademark that is filed with the Trademark Trial and Appeal Board.

arbitrary mark Refers to a mark that, on its face, has nothing to do with the goods or services.

branding Refers to the general category of protection that trademarks fall under.

cancellation Refers to the process of challenging a trademark registration on the principle register.

cease-and-desist letter A letter to a party that is infringing your trademark, instructing them to discontinue such activity.

classifications Refers to headings and categories that are used to group marks for like goods and services.

concurrent use proceeding Refers to a proceeding that occurs when one or more parties are entitled to a concurrent registration to determine the rights of the parties.

cybersquatting This is the bad-faith registration of a domain for profit.

deceptive Refers to a mark that contains a falsity or would be misleading to a consumer purchasing the good or service.

descriptive mark   Refers to a mark that simply describes the good or services.

domain name   Refers to a website address, complete with an extension, which is the ending on a website address. These extensions include the popular *.com*, *.net*, *.org*, and *.edu* but also less popular ones like *.biz*, *.info* and *.ws* (among others).

examining attorney   The person at the U.S. Patent and Trademark Office assigned to review your trademark application.

European Union's Community Trade Mark (CTM)   A system that went into effect in 1996 and allows you to file a single community-wide trademark application.

fanciful marks   Refers to marks that are essentially made-up words and have no relationship to the product or service.

filing receipt   A notification from the USPTO indicating the date, serial number, and other particularities of a received trademark application.

generic term   Refers to a mark or portion of a mark that describes the category of goods or services it falls into such as a dry cleaning service using "Dry Cleaners."

intent-to-use application   Refers to a Trademark Application for a mark that is not currently in use but you have a bona fide intent to use.

interference   Occurs when two or more applicants have conflicting applications for registration.

International Trademark Association (INTA)
Is a nonprofit organization with more than 4,000
members from over 170 different countries.

**Internet Corporation for Assigned Names and
Numbers (ICANN)**   An organization responsible
for managing and coordinating the issuance of
domain names.

licensee   Refers to the individual who is licensing
a mark *from* another person.

licensor   Is the term for the person who is licensing a mark *to* another person.

likelihood of confusion   Refers to when a consumer may think that particular goods or services
are sourced from or associated with a trademark
when in actuality, they are not.

Madrid Protocol   Is an international treaty that
allows a trademark owner to seek registration in
any of the countries that have joined the Madrid
Protocol.

material alteration   Refers to an amendment to a
trademark application that increases the scope of
protection.

nominative fair use   Refers to the use of another
company's mark in connection with describing *their*
goods or services or comparing *their* goods or services to others.

opposition   Refers to the procedure of challenging the registration of a mark before it is registered
by someone that believes they will be harmed if the
mark is registered.

Paris Convention   Was signed into effect in 1883 and a revised version was introduced on July 14, 1967. A primary purpose of the Paris Convention is that it obligates member nations to provide substantive protection for the procurement, maintenance, and enforcement of industrial property.

petition   A process to challenge a position of the examining attorney; the petition is filed with the director of the USPTO.

principle register   Refers to a category of trademark registration for marks that are allowed registration.

priority date   Refers to the date at which your rights in and to a trademark are created.

recordation of assignment   Refers to the filing of an assignment document with the USPTO.

request for consideration   A process that allows you to raise an objection to an examining attorney's refusal in an attempt to have the examining attorney remove the refusal.

scandalous mark   Refers to a mark that is sexually suggestive or is considered profanity.

secondary meaning   A characteristic obtained when the average consumer recognizes or mentally associates the mark with a particular source of goods or services.

service mark   Refers to a word, symbol, logo, groups, or words or designs used to identify services (for example, housecleaning services or restaurants).

statement of use Refers to a written and signed statement indicating that you have now begun use of the trademark.

suggestive marks Refers to marks that are not completely unrelated to the good or service offered, but they're also not completely descriptive.

Supplemental Register Refers to a category of trademark registration for marks that are capable of distinguishing your goods or services, even though the mark may not currently do so and thus cannot currently be registered.

trade dress Refers to the "look and feel" of a good or service and can include trademarks, service marks, and other related items.

trademark Refers to a word, symbol, logo, groups of words, or designs used to identify goods and, sometimes, is generically used to refer to both trademarks and service marks.

Trademark Electronic Application System (TEAS) An online system for filing applications for trademark registration that can be accessed at www.uspto.gov/teas/eTEASpageA.htm.

Trademark Official Gazette A publication by the U.S. government that, among other things, lists the trademarks and service marks, as well as their description of uses.

Trademark Trial and Appeal Board A group that hears and decides adversary proceedings involving: oppositions to the registration of

trademarks, petitions to cancel trademark registrations, and proceedings involving applications for concurrent use registrations of trademarks.

use in commerce   Refers to a business activity that occurs between states or between a state and a foreign country.

use-based application   An application for a trademark that is currently being used in commerce.

World Intellectual Property Organization (WIPO)   Is an administrative arm of the United Nations to support international trade and to promote reciprocity of IP recognition and protection among various nations.

Index

A

abandoning trademarks, 108-109

Acceptable Identification of Goods and Services Manual, 53-54

ACPA (Anticybersquatting Consumer Protection Act), 122

Affidavits of Continued Use, filing, 103-107

affixation, marks, 4-5

African Intellectual Property Organisation (AIPO), 159

African Regional Industrial Property Organization (ARIPO), 149, 158

AIPLA (American Intellectual Property Law Association), 177

AIPO (African Intellectual Property Organisation), 149, 159

amendments, application filings, 83-84

American Express, 22

American Intellectual Property Law Association (AIPLA), 177

Anticybersquatting Consumer Protection Act (ACPA), 122

appeals, applications, 89

applicant information (applications), filling out, 63-64

applications, 61-62
  appeals, 89
  compliance, 89
  examination stage, 47-48
  examinations, 80
  examining attorneys, 85
  oppositions, 94, 96
  petitions for cancellation, 96
  petitions to the director, 93-94
  refusals, 88-89
  reviews, 85-87
  TTAB (Trademark Trial and Appeals Board), 90-93

filing, 47, 74
  by mail, 76-77
  confirmations, 80
  dates, 82
  errors, 81-82
  fees, 68
  online, 74-76
  preliminary amendments, 83-84
  receipts, 82

filling out, 63-65, 67-70
  applicant information, 63-64
  authorized signatures, 69
  correspondence address, 67
  trademark information, 64
  use of the trademark, 66

foreign registration-based applications, 63
  filling out, 72-74

intent-to-use applications, 62
  assigning, 138
  filling out, 71-72

international trademarks
  filing, 143-154
  processing, 154-160

issuance stage, 49

monitoring, 97

petitions, 89

publication stage, 48

request reconsiderations, 89
specimen submissions, 69
use-based applications, 62
filling out, 70-71
arbitrary marks, 15
ARIPO (African Regional Industrial Property Organization), 149, 158
assignments, 162
assignments of ownership, changing, 138
attorneys
choosing, 181-184
cost considerations, 183
examining attorneys, applications, 85-96
response times, 182
trademark registrations, 179, 181

B-C

BAND-AID, 115
branding, 2-3
generic terms, 22
trade dress, 3-4
brands, protecting, 6, 8-9
buildings, trademarking, 27
businesses, naming, 13-17

Cabbage Patch Kids, 41
cancellation of certification marks, 113
cancellation of registrations, 110-112
cease and desist letters, 38-40
certification marks, cancellation of, 113
classes, trademarks, 52-54
clearance searches, 178
Coca-Cola, 25-26, 30
invention of, 100
colors, trademarking, 27
community trademarks, 176
companies, naming, 13-17
compliance, applications, 89
confirmations, filings, 80

confusion
avoiding, 102
determining, 103
consumer protection, 9
copyrights, 2
trademarks, compared, 11
corporate exploitation, 10
corporate names, trademarks, compared, 16
cost to replace valuation method, licensing, 170
cybersquatting, domain names, 121-122

D-E

dates, filings, 82
descriptive marks, 19, 24
suggestive marks, compared, 19-20
design marks, 25-26
dilution of trademarks, 115
discontinued use of trademarks, 108-109
disputes, domain names, 124-128
Domain Direct, 179
domain names, 117-118
cybersquatting, 121-122
disputes, 124-128
online resources, 179
parodies, 123-124
registering as trademarks, 119-120
trademarks, compared, 118

eCompanies, 121
employers, intellectual property rights, 134-135
errors, filings, 81-82
European Union's Community Trade Mark (CTM) system, 148, 158
examination stage, trademark applications, 47-48
examinations, applications, 80

examining attorneys, applications, 85
  oppositions, 94, 96
  petitions for cancellation, 96
  petitions to the director, 93-94
  refusals, 88-89
  reviews, 85-87
  TTAB (Trademark Trial and Appeals Board), 90, 92-93
expansion, ownership rights, 132-134

F

famous marks, infringement, 34
fanciful marks, 15
federal registration, marks, 7-8
  USPTO (United States Patent and Trademark Office), 8
fees, renewals, 106-107
filing
  Affidavits of Continued Use, 103-106
    fees, 106-107
  applications, 74
    by mail, 76-77
    confirmations, 80
    errors, 81-82
    international trademarks, 143-147, 149-154
    online, 74-76
    preliminary amendments, 83-84
    receipts, 82
  trademark applications, 47
Flopps, 42
foreign registration-based applications, 63
  filling out, 63-74
foreign trademarks, 58, 60
  applications
    filing, 143-154
    processing, 154-160
  searching for, 59

G

Garbage Pail Kids, 41
generic terms, branding, 22
generic trademarks, 113-115
  becoming, 103, 109-110
geographic names, 21
geographic rights, marks, 36-37
GoDaddy.com, 179
goods, services, compared, 49, 51-52
government agencies, online resources, 174
group filings, foreign trademarks, 146-147

H-I

Hewlett-Packard, 20
Home Depot, 25

ICANN (Internet Corporation for Assigned Names and Numbers), 120, 179
  domain names, disputes, 124-128
income valuation method, licensing, 170
individual country filings, foreign trademarks, 145-146
infringement, 31
  cease and desist letters, 38-40
  geographic issues, 35-37
  likelihood of confusion
    discerning, 32-33
    proving, 33-36
  parodies, 41
INTA (International Trademark Association), 177
intangibles values, 171
intellectual properties, protecting, 12, 162
Intent-to-Use trademark applications, 6

intent-to-use applications, 62
  assigning, 138
  examinations, 80
  examining attorneys, 85
    oppositions, 94, 96
    petitions for cancellation, 96
    petitions to the director, 93-94
    refusals, 88-89
    reviews, 85-87
    TTAB (Trademark Trial and Appeals Board), 90, 92-93
  filing
    confirmations, 80
    dates, 82
    errors, 81-82
    preliminary amendments, 83-84
    receipts, 82
  filling out, 63-65, 67-72
  monitoring, 97
interbrand approach, trademark licensing, 171
International Trademark Association (INTA), 177
international trademarks, 142-143, 177
  applications
    filing, 143-154
    processing, 154-160
Internet
  applications, monitoring, 97
  domain names, 117-118
    cybersquatting, 121-122
    disputes, 124-128
    parodies, 123-124
    registering as trademarks, 119-120
  marks, geographic issues, 37
  resources, 174-176, 179
Internet Corporation for Assigned Names and Numbers (ICANN), 120
inures, 132
issuance stage, trademarks, 49

J–K–L

Johnson & Johnson, 20
  BAND-AIDs, 115
joint ownership, 136-137

Kodak, 15

Lanham Act, 6, 8
  secondary meanings, 19
Lanham, Fritz Garland, 8
last names, marks, 20
LawMart, 178
lawyers. *See* attorneys, 183
licensing, trademarks, 162-169
  interbrand approach, 171
  pure-profit licensing, 171-172
  valuation methods, 170
likelihood of confusion, 31
  discerning, 32-33
  proving, 33-36
logos, 25-26

M

Madrid Agreement Concerning the International Registration of Marks, 151
Madrid Protocol, 151-157
  foreign trademark group filings, 147
market valuation method, licensing, 170
marks
  affixation, 4-5
  arbitrary marks, 15
  buildings, 27
  changing, 23
  classes, 52-54
  colors, 27
  copyrights, compared, 11
  corporate names, compared, 16
  creating, 13-17
  descriptive marks, 19-20, 24
  fanciful marks, 15
  foreign trademarks, 58, 60
  geographic issues, 35-37

geographic terms, 21
infringement, cease and
  desist letters, 38-40
last names, 20
licensing, 162-169
    interbrand approach,
      171
    pure-profit licensing,
      171-172
    valuation methods, 170
likelihood of confusion, 31
    discerning, 32-33
    proving, 33-36
logos, 25-26
ownership
    expansion of, 132-134
    requirements, 130-131
ownership rights, 31-32
parodies of, 41-42
patents, compared, 11-12
prohibited marks, 23-24
protecting, 6, 8-9
registering, 43-46
    before use, 54, 56
    examination stage,
      47-48
    federal registration, 7-8
    issuance stage, 49
    publication stage, 48
    use in commerce, 7
    USPTO (United States
      Patent and Trademark
      Office), 8
reserving, 6
scents, 27
secondary meanings, 18-19
shapes, 26
slogans, 22
sounds, 26
state law protection, 7
stylized marks, 25
suggestive marks, 16,
  19-20
symbols, 17
usage, 5
using someone else's, 40-41
MasterCard, 16
material alteration amendments, 84
McDonald's, 4, 22

Microsoft, 30
monitoring applications, 97

N-O

Nairobi Treaty, 160
names
    changing, 23
    reserving, 6
NFL Pro-Set, 42
Nike, 22, 25
non-famous marks, 26
    infringement, 35

Office of Harmonization in
  the Internal Market
  (OHIM), 176
Official Gazette, 48
OHIM (Office of
  Harmonization in the
  Internal Market), 176
online resources, 174-176, 179
oppositions, applications, 94,
  96
ownership
    employer's rights, 134-135
    expansion of, 132-134
    joint ownership, 136-137
    reassigning, 137-140
    requirements, 130-131
    single-entity ownership,
      135-136
ownership rights
    registrations, compared,
      43, 45-46
    trademarks, 31-32

P-Q

Paris Convention, 150
parodies
    domain names, 123-124
    trademarks, 41-42
patents, 2
    trademarks, compared,
      11-12
Pemberton, John S., 99

petitions, applications, 89
petitions for cancellation, applications, 96
petitions to the director, applications, 93-94
preliminary amendments, filings, 83-84
principle registrations, 56-57
  supplemental registrations, changing from, 58
Pro-Set, 42
processing, applications, international trademarks, 154-160
profane marks, 24
protection, ownership, span of protection, 101-103
protections
  consumer protection, 9
  corporate exploitation, 10
publishing, trademarks, 48
pure-profit licensing, 171-172

R

reassigning trademarks, 137-140
receipts, filings, 82
references, attorneys, 181
refusals, applications
  examining attorneys, 88-89
  oppositions, 94, 96
  petitions for cancellation, 96
  petitions to the director, 93-94
  TTAB (Trademark Trial and Appeals Board), 90, 92-93
Register.com, 179
registrars, 120
registration
  cancellation of certification marks, 113
  cancellation of registrations, 110-112

domain names, 119-120
  cybersquatting, 121-122
marks
  federal registration, 7-8
  USPTO (United States Patent and Trademark Office), 8
ownership rights, expansion of, 133-134
renewals, 105-106
  fees, 106-107
trademarks, before use, 54, 56
registrations
  attorneys, 179, 181
  ownership rights, compared, 43, 45-46
  principle registrations, 56-57
    changing to, 58
  process
    examination stage, 47-48
    filing stage, 47
    issuance stage, 49
    publication stage, 48
  supplemental registrations, 57-58
renewing, trademarks, 103-106
  fees, 106-107
request reconsiderations, applications, 89
response times, attorneys, 182
reviews, applications, 85-87
rights, ownership
  employers, 134-135
  expansion of, 132-134
  joint ownership, 136-137
  marks, 31-32
  reassigning, 137-140
  requirements, 130-131
  single-entity ownership, 135-136
  span of protection, 101-103
registration mark, ®, 17
Robinson, Frank, 99

S

scandalous marks, 24
scents, trademarking, 27
Sears, 20
secondary meanings, 18-19
    descriptive marks, 19-20
    geographic terms, 21
    last names, 20
    slogans, 22
    suggestive marks, 19-20
service marks, 3
services, goods, compared,
    49, 51-52
shapes, marks, 26
single-entity ownership,
    135-136
slogans, trademarking, 22
SM (service mark) symbol,
    17
sounds, trademarking, 26
span of protection, trade-
    marks, 101-103
specimen submissions,
    applications, 69
stylized marks, 25
suggestive marks, 16
    descriptive marks, com-
        pared, 19-20
supplemental registrations,
    57-58
    principle registrations,
        changing to, 58
symbols, 17

T

TEAS (Trademark
    Electronic Application
    System), 74-76
Thomson & Thomson, 178
TiVo, 15
TM (trademark) symbol, 17
Topps, 42
trade dress, 3-4
Trademark Electronic
    Application System
    (TEAS), 75

Trademark Official Gazette, 48
Trademark Trial and Appeal
    Board (TTAB), 90
trademarks, 1
    affixation, 4-5
    arbitrary marks, 15
    buildings, 27
    changing, 23
    classes, 52-54
    colors, 27
    copyrights, compared, 11
    corporate names, compared,
        16
    creating, 13-17
    descriptive marks, 19-20, 24
    fanciful marks, 15
    foreign trademarks, 58-60
    geographic issues, 35-37
    geographic terms, 21
    infringement, cease and
        desist letters, 38-40
    last names, 20
    licensing, 162-169
        interbrand approach,
            171
        pure-profit licensing,
            171-172
        valuation methods, 170
    likelihood of confusion, 31
        discerning, 32-33
        proving, 33-36
    logos, 25-26
    ownership, 31-32
        expansion of, 132-134
        requirements, 130-131
    parodies of, 41-42
    patents, compared, 11-12
    prohibited marks, 23-24
    protecting, 6, 8-9
    registering, 43, 45-46
        before use, 54, 56
        examination stage, 47-48
        federal registration, 7-8
        filing stage, 47
        issuance stage, 49
        publication stage, 48
        use in commerce, 7
        USPTO (United States
            Patent and Trademark
            Office), 8

reserving, 6
scents, 27
secondary meanings, 18-19
shapes, 26
slogans, 22
sounds, 26
state law protection, 7
stylized marks, 25
suggestive marks, 16, 19-20
symbols, 17
usage, 5
using someone else's, 40-41
TTAB (Trademark Trial and Appeals Board), 90, 92-93

U

United States Patent and Trademark Office (USPTO). *See* USPTO
use in commerce (mark registration), 7
use-based applications, 62
examinations, 80
examining attorneys, 85
oppositions, 94, 96
petitions for cancellation, 96
petitions to the director, 93-94
refusals, 88-89
reviews, 85-87
TTAB (Trademark Trial and Appeals Board), 90, 92-93
filing
confirmations, 80
dates, 82
errors, 81-82
preliminary amendments, 83-84
receipts, 82

filling out, 63-71
monitoring, 97
USPTO (United States Patent and Trademark Office)
applications, monitoring, 97
TEAS (Trademark Electronic Application System), 75
registering with, 8
website, 174

V-W-X-Y-Z

valuation methods, trademark licensing, 170
Verio.com, 179
Verisign.com, 179
Visomark, 178

websites
domain names, 117-118
cybersquatting, 121-122
disputes, 124-128
parodies, 123-124
registering as trademarks, 119-120
resources, 174-176, 179
Wendy's, 4
WIPO (World Intellectual Property Organization), 149
website, 176

Xerox, 15, 114

Yahoo!, 14-15